A Short History of The Book of Common Prayer

William Reed Huntington

Copyright © BiblioLife, LLC

BiblioLife Reproduction Series: Our goal at BiblioLife is to help readers, educators and researchers by bringing back in print hard-to-find original publications at a reasonable price and, at the same time, preserve the legacy of literary history. The following book represents an authentic reproduction of the text as printed by the original publisher and may contain prior copyright references. While we have attempted to accurately maintain the integrity of the original work(s), from time to time there are problems with the original book scan that may result in minor errors in the reproduction, including imperfections such as missing and blurred pages, poor pictures, markings and other reproduction issues beyond our control. Because this work is culturally important, we have made it available as a part of our commitment to protecting, preserving and promoting the world's literature.

All of our books are in the "public domain" and some are derived from Open Source projects dedicated to digitizing historic literature. We believe that when we undertake the difficult task of re-creating them as attractive, readable and affordable books, we further the mutual goal of sharing these works with a larger audience. A portion of BiblioLife profits go back to Open Source projects in the form of a donation to the groups that do this important work around the world. If you would like to make a donation to these worthy Open Source projects, or would just like to get more information about these important initiatives, please visit www.bibliolife.com/opensource.

A SHORT HISTORY

OF

THE BOOK OF COMMON PRAYER

TOGETHER WITH

CERTAIN PAPERS ILLUSTRATIVE OF
LITURGICAL REVISION 1878-1892

BY

WILLIAM REED HUNTINGTON D. D. D. C. L.
Rector of Grace Church New York

NEW YORK
THOMAS WHITTAKER
2 AND 3 BIBLE HOUSE

Copyright, 1893,
by
THOMAS WHITTAKER.

THE MERSHON COMPANY PRESS,
RAHWAY, N. J.

CONTENTS.

	PAGE
I. A SHORT HISTORY OF THE BOOK OF COMMON PRAYER:	
I. ORIGINS,	3
II. VICISSITUDES,	20
II. REVISION OF THE AMERICAN COMMON PRAYER,	61
III. THE BOOK ANNEXED: ITS CRITICS AND ITS PROSPECTS,	133
APPENDIX:	
I. PERMANENT AND VARIABLE CHARACTERISTICS OF THE PRAYER BOOK—A SERMON BEFORE REVISION, 1878,	213
II. THE OUTCOME OF REVISION, 1892,	228
III. TABULAR VIEW OF ADDITIONS MADE AT THE SUCCESSIVE REVISIONS, 1552-1892,	235

INTRODUCTORY NOTE.

THE opening paper of this collection was originally read as a lecture before a liturgical class, and is now published for the first time. The others have appeared in print from time to time during the movement for revision. If they have any permanent value, it is because of their showing, so far as the writer's part in the matter is concerned, what things were attempted and what things failed of accomplishment. Should they serve as contributory to some future narrative of the revision, the object of their publication will have been accomplished. So much has been said as to the poverty of our gains on the side of "enrichment," as compared with what has been secured in the line of "flexibility," that it has seemed proper to append to the volume a COMPARATIVE TABLE detailing the additions of liturgical matter made to the Common Prayer at the successive revisions.   W. R. H.

NEW YORK, Christmas, 1892.

A SHORT HISTORY OF THE BOOK OF COMMON PRAYER.

A SHORT HISTORY OF THE BOOK OF COMMON PRAYER.

I

ORIGINS.

LITURGICAL worship, understood in the largest sense the phrase can bear, means divine service rendered in accordance with an established form. Of late years there has been an attempt made among purists to confine the word "liturgy" to the office entitled in the Prayer Book, *The Order for the Administration of the Lord's Supper or Holy Communion*.

This restricted and specialized interpretation of a familiar word may serve the purposes of technical scholarship, for undoubtedly there is much to be said in favor of the narrowed signification as we shall see ; but unless English literature can be rewritten, plain people who draw their vocabulary from standard authors will go on calling service-books "liturgies" regardless of the fact that they contain many things other than that one office which is entitled to be named by eminence *the* Liturgy. "This Convention," write the fathers of the American Episcopal Church in the Ratification printed on the fourth page of the Prayer Book, "having in their present session set forth a Book of Common Prayer and other rites and ceremonies of the Church, do hereby establish the said book ; and they declare it to be the *Liturgy* of this Church."

For the origin of liturgy thus broadly defined we have to go a long way back ; beyond the Prayer Book, beyond the Mass-book, beyond the ancient Sacramentaries, yes, beyond the synagogue worship, beyond the temple worship, beyond the tabernacle worship; in fact I am disposed to think that, logically, we should be unable to stop short until we had reached the very heart of man itself, that dimly discerned groundwork we call human nature, and had discovered there those two instincts, the one of worship and the other of gregariousness, from whence all forms of common prayer have sprung. Where three or two assemble for the purposes of supplication, some form must necessarily be accepted if they are to pray in unison. When the disciples came to Jesus begging him that he would teach them how to pray, he gave them, not twelve several forms, though doubtless James's special needs differed from John's and Simon's from Jude's—he gave them, not twelve, but one. "When ye pray," was his answer, "say Our Father." That was the beginning of Christian Common Prayer. Because we are men we worship, because we are fellow-men our worship must have form.

But waiving this last analysis of all which carries us across the whole field of history at a leap, it becomes necessary to seek for liturgical beginnings by a more plodding process.

If we take that manual of worship with which as English-speaking Christians we are ourselves the most familiar, the Book of Common Prayer, and allow it to fall naturally apart, as a bunch of flowers would do if the string were cut, we discover that in point of fact we have, as in the case of the Bible, many books in one. We have scarcely turned the title-page, for instance, before we come upon a ritual of daily worship, an order for Morning Prayer and an order for Evening Prayer, consisting in the main of Psalms, Scripture Lessons, Antiphonal Versicles, and Collects. Appended to this we find a Litany or General Supplication and a collection of special prayers.

Mark an interval here, and note that we have completed the first volume of our liturgical library. Next, we have a sacramental ritual, entitled, *The Order for the Administration of the Lord's Supper or Holy Communion*, ingeniously interwoven by a system of appropriate prayers and New Testament readings with the Sundays and holydays of the year. This gives us our second volume. Then follow numerous offices which we shall find it convenient to classify under two heads, namely: those which may be said by a bishop or by a presbyter, and those that may be said by a bishop only. Under the former head come the baptismal offices, the Order for the Burial of the Dead, and the like; under the latter, the services of Ordination and Confirmation and the Form of Consecration of a Church or Chapel.

In the Church of England as it existed before the Reformation, these four volumes, as I have called them, were distinct and recognized realities. Each had its title and each its separate use. The name of the book of daily services was *The Breviary*. The name of the book used in the celebration of the Holy Communion was *The Missal*. The name of the book of Special Offices was *The Ritual*. The name of the book of such offices as could be used by a bishop only was *The Pontifical*. It was one of the greatest of the achievements of the English reformers that they succeeded in condensing, after a practical fashion, these four books, or, to speak more accurately, the first three of them, Breviary, Missal, and Ritual, into one. The Pontifical, or Ordinal, they continued as a separate book, although it soon for the sake of convenience became customary in England, as it has always been customary here, for Prayer Book and Ordinal to be stitched together by the binders into a single volume. Popularly speaking the Prayer Book is the entire volume one purchases under that name from the bookseller, but accurately speaking the Book of Common Prayer ends where *The Form and Manner of Making, Ordaining, and Consecrating Bishops, Priests, and Deacons* begins. "Finis" should be written after the Psalter, as indeed from the Prayer Book's Table of Contents plainly appears.

Setting aside now, for the present, that portion of the formularies which corresponds to the Ritual and Pontifical of the mediæval Church, I proceed to speak rapidly of the antecedents of Breviary and Missal. Whence came they? And how are we to account for their being sundered so distinctly as they are?

They came, so some of the most thoughtful of liturgical students are agreed, from a source no less remote than the Temple of Solomon, and they are severed, to speak figuratively, by a valley not unlike that which in our thoughts divides the Mount of Beatitudes from the Hill of Calvary.

In that memorable building to which reference was just made, influential over the destinies of our race as no other house of man's making ever was, there went on from day to day these two things, psalmody and sacrifice. Peace-offering, burnt-offering, sin-offering, the morning oblation, and the evening oblation—these with other ceremonies of a like character went to make what we know as the sacrificial ritual of the temple.

But this was not all. It would appear that there were other services in the temple over and above those that could strictly be called sacrificial. The Hebrew Psalter, the hymn-book of that early day, contains much that was evidently intended by the writers for temple use, and even more that could be easily adapted to such use. And although there is no direct evidence that in Solomon's time forms of prayer other than those associated with sacrificial rites were in use, yet when we find mention in the New Testament of people going up to the temple of those later days "at the hour of prayer," it seems reasonable to infer that the custom was an ancient one, and that from the beginning of the temple's history forms of worship not strictly speaking sacrificial had been a stated feature of the ritual. But whether in the temple or not, certainly in the synagogues, which after the return from the captivity sprang up all over the Jewish world, services composed of prayers, of psalms, and of readings from the law and the prophets were of continual occurrence. Therefore we may safely say that with these two forms of divine service, the sacrificial and the simply devotional and didactic, the apostles, the founders of the Christian Church, had been familiar from their childhood. They were at home in both synagogue and temple. They knew by sight the ritual of the altar, and by ear the ritual of the choir. They were accustomed to the spectacle of the priest offering the victim; they were used to hearing the singers chant the psalms.

We see thus why it is that the public worship of the Church should have come down to us in two great lines, why there should be a tradition of eucharistic worship and, parallel to this, a tradition of daily prayer; for as the one usage links itself, in a sense, to the sacrificial system of God's ancient people and has in it a suggestion of the temple worship, so the other seems to show a continuity with what went on in those less pretentious sanctuaries which had place in all the cities and villages of Judea, and indeed wherever, throughout the Roman world, Jewish colonists were to be found. The earliest Christian disciples having been themselves Hebrews, nothing could have been more natural than their moulding the worship of the new Church in general accordance with the models that had stood before their eyes from childhood in the old. The Psalms were sung in the synagogues according to a settled principle. We cannot wonder, then, that the Psalter should have continued to be what in fact it had always been, the hymn-book of the Church. Moreover, they had in the synagogue besides their psalmody a system of Bible readings, confined, of course, to the Old Testament Scriptures. This is noted in the observation that fell from Simon Peter, at the first Council of the Church, "Moses of old time hath in every city them that preach him, being read in the synagogue every Sabbath day." Scripture lessons, therefore, would be no novelty.

We gather also from the New Testament, not to speak of other authorities, that in the apostolic days people were familiar with what were known as "hours of prayer." There were particular times in the day, that is to say, which were held to be especially appropriate for worship. "Peter and John went up together into the temple at the hour of prayer, being the ninth hour." Again, at Joppa, we find the former of these two apostles going up upon the house-top to pray at "the sixth hour." Long before this David had mentioned morning and evening and noon as fitting hours of prayer, and one psalmist, in his enthusiasm, had even gone so far as to declare *seven* times a day to be not too often for giving God thanks. There was also the precedent of Daniel opening his windows toward Jerusalem three times a day. As the love for order and system grew year by year stronger in the Christian Church, the laws that govern ritual would be likely to become more stringent, and so very probably it came to pass. For aught we know to the contrary, the observance of fixed hours of prayer was a matter of voluntary action with the Christians of the first age. There was, as we say, no "shall" about it. But when the founders of the monastic orders came upon the scene a fixed rule took the place of simple custom, and what had been optional became mandatory. By the time we reach the mediæval period evolution has had its perfect work, and we find in existence a scheme of daily service curiously and painfully elaborate. The mediæval theologians were very fond of classifying things by sevens. In the symbolism of Holy Scripture seven appears as the number of perfection, it being the aggregate of three, the number of Deity, and four, the number of the earth. Accordingly we find in the theology of those times seven sacraments, seven deadly sins, seven contrary virtues, seven works of mercy, and also seven hours of prayer. These seven hours were known as Matins, Prime, Tierce, Sext, Nones, Vespers, and Complene. The theory of the hours of prayer was that at each one of them a special office of devotion was to be said. Beginning before sunrise with matins there was to be daily a round of services at stated intervals culminating at bedtime in that which, as its name indicated, filled out the series, Complene. To what extent this ideal scheme of devotion was ever carried out in practice it is difficult positively to say.

Probably in the monastic and conventual life of the severer orders there was an approximation to a punctual observance of the hours as they successively arrived. Possibly the modern mind fails to do full justice to the conception of worship on which this system was based. Those principles of devotion of which the rosary is the visible symbol do not easily commend themselves to us. They have about them a suggestion of mechanism. They remind us of the Buddhist praying wheel, and seem to put the Church in the attitude of expecting to be heard for her "much speaking."

Doubtless many a pure, courageous spirit fought the good fight of faith successfully in spite of all this weight of outward observances; but in the judgment of the wiser heads among English churchmen, the time had come, by the middle of the sixteenth century, when this complicated armor must either be greatly lightened or else run the risk of being cast aside altogether. Let Cranmer tell his own story. This is what he says in the Preface to the First Book of Edward VI. as to the ritual grievances of the times. The passage is worth listening to if only for the quaintness of its strong and wholesome English :

"There was never anything by the wit of man so well devised or so surely established which, in continuance of time, hath not been corrupted, as, among other things, it may plainly appear by the common prayer, in the Church, commonly called divine service. The first original and ground whereof, if a man would search out by the ancient fathers, he shall find that the same was not ordained but of a good purpose, and for a great advancement of godliness, for they so ordered the matter that all the whole Bible, or the greatest part thereof, should be read over once in the year. . . But these many years past this godly and decent order of the ancient fathers hath been so altered, broken, and neglected by planting in uncertain stories, legends, responds, verses, vain repetitions, commemorations, and synodals that commonly, when any book of the Bible was begun, before three or four chapters were read out all the rest were unread. And in this sort the Book of Esaie was begun in Advent, and the Book of Genesis in Septuagesima, but they were only begun and never read through. . . And moreover, whereas St. Paul would have such language spoken to the people in the Church as they might understand and have profit by hearing the same, the service in this Church of England (these many years) hath been read in Latin to the people, which they understood not, so that they have heard with their ears only, and their hearts, spirit, and mind have not been edified thereby. . . Moreover, the number and hardness of the rules called the Pie, and the manifold changings of the service was the cause that to turn the Book only was so hard and intricate a matter that many times there was more business to find out what should be read than it was to read it when it was found out. These inconveniences therefore considered, here is set forth such an order whereby the same shall be redressed."

As an illustration of what Cranmer meant by his curious phrase, "planting in uncertain stories," take the following Lessons quoted by Dr. Neale in his *Essays on Liturgiology*:

"Besides the commemoration of saints," writes this distinguished antiquarian, "there are in certain local calenders notices of national events connected with the well-being of the Church. Thus, in the *Parisian Breviary*, we have on the eighteenth of August a commemoration of the victory of Philip the Fair in Flanders, A. D. 1304." Here is the fourth of the appointed lessons: " Philip the Fair, King of the French, in the year 1304, about the feast of St. Mary Magdalene, having set forth with his brothers Charles and Louis and a large army into Flanders, pitched his tent near Mons, where was a camp of the rebel Flemings. But when, on the eighteenth of August, which was the Tuesday after the Assumption of St. Mary, the French had from morning till evening stood on the defence, and were resting themselves at nightfall, the enemy, by a sudden attack, rushed on the camp with such fury that the body-guard had scarce time to defend him.

"*Response*. Come from Lebanon, my spouse; come, and thou shalt be crowned. The odor of thy sweet ointments is above all perfumes. *Versicle*. The righteous judge shall give a crown of righteousness."

Then, after this short interlude of snatches from Holy Scripture, there follows the Fifth Lesson: "At the beginning of the fight the life of the king was in great danger, but shortly after, his troops crowding together from all quarters to his tent, where the battle was sharpest, obtained an illustrious victory over the enemy"—and more of this sort until all of a sudden we come upon the Song of Solomon again "*V.* Thou art all fair, my love; come from Lebanon. *R.* They that have not defiled their garments, they shall walk with me in white, for they are worthy."

Is not Cranmer's contemptuous mention of these uncertain legends and vain repetitions amply justified? And can we be too thankful to the sturdy champions of the Reformation, who in the face of no little opposition and by efforts scarcely appreciated to-day, cut us loose from all responsibility for such solemn nonsense?

There are some who feel aggrieved that chapters from the Apocrypha should have found admission to our new lectionary, and there are even those who think that of the canonical Scriptures, passages more edifying than certain of those appointed to be read might have been chosen, but what would they think if they were compelled to hear the minister at the lectern say: "Here beginneth the first chapter of the Adventures of Philip the Fair"?

But the reformers, happily, were not discouraged by the portentous front of wood, hay, and stubble which the liturgical edifice of their day presented to the eye. They felt convinced that there were also to be found mixed in with the building material gold, silver, and precious stones, and for these they determined to make diligent search, resolved most of all that the foundation laid should be Jesus Christ. This system of canonical hours, they argued, this seven-fold office of daily prayer is all very beautiful in theory, but it never can be made what in fact it never in the past has been, a practicable thing. Let us be content if we can do so much as win people to their devotions at morning and at night. With this object in view Cranmer and his associates subjected the services of the hours to a process of combination and condensation. The Offices for the first three hours they compressed into *An Order for Daily Morning Prayer*, or, as it was called in Edward's first Book, *An Order for Matins*, and the Offices for the last two hours, namely, Vespers and Complene, they made over into *An Order for Daily Evening Prayer*, or, as it was named in Edward's first Book, *An Order for Evensong*.

These two formularies, the *Order for Matins* and the *Order for Evensong*, make the core and substance of our present daily offices. But the tradition of daily prayer is only one of the two great devotional heritages of the Church. With the destruction of the temple by the Roman soldiery, the sacrificial ritual of the Jewish Church came to a sudden end; but it was not God's purpose that the memory of sacrifice should fade out of men's minds or that the thought of sacrifice should be banished from the field of worship. Years before the day when the legionaries of Titus marched amid flame and smoke, into the falling sanctuary of an out-worn faith, one who was presently to die upon a cross had taken bread, had blessed it and broken it, and giving it to certain followers gathered about him, had said, "Take, eat; this is my body, which is given for you: this do in remembrance of me." Likewise also he had taken the cup after supper, saying, "This cup is the New Testament in my blood which is shed for you."

Certainly there must be a relation of cause and effect between this scene and the fact, which is a fact, that the most ancient fragments of primitive Christian worship now discoverable are forms for the due commemoration of the sacrifice of the death of Christ.

These venerable monuments seem to exclaim as we decipher them: "Even so, Lord, it is done as thou didst say." "Thy name, O Lord, endureth forever and so doth thy memorial from generation to generation." Of the references to Christian worship discoverable in documents later than the New Testament Scriptures there are three that stand out with peculiar prominence, namely, the lately discovered *Teaching of the Twelve Apostles*, placed by some authorities as early as the first half of the second century; the famous letter of Pliny to the Emperor Trajan, a writing of the same period; and the Apology or Defence addressed by Justin Martyr to Antoninus Pius about the year 140 after Christ. The noteworthy fact in connection with these passages is that of the three, two certainly, and probably the third also, refer directly to the Holy Communion. In the *Teaching* we have a distinct sketch of a eucharistic service with three of the prescribed prayers apparently given in full. In Justin Martyr's account, the evidence of a definitely established liturgical form is perhaps less plain, but nothing that he says would appear to be irreconcilable with the existence of a more or less elastic ritual order. Whether he does or does not intend to describe extemporaneous prayer as forming one feature of the eucharistic worship of the Christians of his time depends upon the translation we give to a single word in his narrative. Later on in the life of the Church, though by just how much later is a difficult point of scholarship, we are brought in contact with a number of formularies, all of them framed for the uses of eucharistical worship, all of them, that is to say, designed to perpetuate the commandment, "This do in remembrance of me," and all of them preserving, no matter in what part of the world they may be found, a certain structural uniformity. These are the primitive liturgies, as they are called, the study of which has in late years attained almost to the dignity of a science.

As to the exact measure of antiquity that ought to be accorded to these venerable documents the authorities differ and probably will always differ. Dr. Neale's enthusiasm carried him so far that he was persuaded and sought to persuade others of the existence of liturgical quotations in the writings of St. Paul. This hypothesis is at the present time generally rejected by sober-minded scholars. Perhaps "the personal equation" enters equally into the conclusions of those who assign a very late origin to the liturgies, pushing them along as far as the sixth or seventh century. If one happens to have a rooted dislike for prescribed forms of worship, and believes them in his heart to be both unscriptural and unspiritual, it will be the most natural thing in the world for him to disparage whatever evidence makes in favor of the early origin of liturgies. Hammond is sensible when he says in the Preface to his valuable work entitled

Liturgies Eastern and Western, "I have assumed an intermediate position between the views of those on the one hand who hold that the liturgies had assumed a recognized and fixed form so early as to be quoted in the Epistles to the Corinthians and Hebrews . . . and of those, on the other, who because there are some palpable interpolations and marks of comparatively late date in some of the texts, assert broadly that they are *all* untrustworthy and valueless as evidence. This view I venture to think," he adds, " equally uncritical and groundless with the former."

To sum up, the argument in behalf of an apostolic origin for the Christian Liturgy may be compactly stated thus : The very earliest monuments of Christian worship that we possess are rituals of thanksgiving, having direct reference to the sacrifice of the death of Christ. Going back from these to the New Testament we find there the narrative of the institution of the Holy Communion by Christ himself, and in connection with it the command, " This do in remembrance of me." It is, I submit, a reasonable inference that the liturgies in the main fairly represent what it was in the mind of the apostle to recognize and establish as proper Christian worship. I do not call it demonstration, I call it reasonable inference. There is a striking parallelism between the argument for liturgical worship and the argument for episcopacy. In both cases we take the ground that continuity existed between the life of the Church as we find it a hundred years after the last of the apostles had gone to his rest and the life of the Church as it is pictured in the New Testament.

That there were many changes during the interval

must no doubt be granted, but we say that if those changes were serious ones affecting great principles of belief or order, those who maintain that such a hidden revolution took place are bound to bring positive evidence to the fact. This history of the Church during the second century has been likened with more of ingenuity than of poetical beauty to the passing of a train through a railway tunnel.

We see the train enter, we see it emerge, but its movement while inside the tunnel is concealed from us. Similarly we may say that we see with comparative distinctness the Christian Church of the Apostolic Age, and we see with comparative distinctness the Church of the Age of Cyprian and Origen, but with respect to the interval separating the two periods we are not indeed wholly, but, we are, it must be confessed, very largely ignorant. And yet as in the case of the tunnel we confidently affirm an identity between what we saw go in and what we see coming out, so with the doctrine, discipline, and worship of the Church, the usages of the third century, we argue, are probably in their leading features what the usages of the first century were. If reason to the contrary can be given, well and good; but in the absence of countervailing testimony we abide by our inference, holding it to be sound.

I am far from wishing to maintain that these considerations bind liturgical worship upon the Christian Church as a matter of obligation for all time. It might be argued, and I think with great force, that liturgical worship having been universal throughout the ancient world, heathen as well as Jewish, the apostles and fathers of the Christian Church judged it unwise to make any departure at the outset from a custom so invariable, trusting it to the spirit of the new religion to work out freer and less formal methods of approaching God through Christ in the times to come. This, I confess, strikes me as a perfectly legitimate line of reasoning and one which is strengthened rather than weakened by what we have seen happen in Christendom since the sixteenth century. Great bodies of Christians have for a period of some three hundred years been worshipping Almighty God in non-liturgical ways, and have not been left without witness that their service was acceptable to the Divine Majesty. Moreover, the fact that absolute rigidity in liturgical use never was insisted upon in any age of the Church until the English passed their Act of Uniformity, makes in the same direction. And yet even after these allowances have been made, there remains a considerable amount of solid satisfaction for those who do adhere to the liturgical method, in the thought that they are in the line which is apparently the line of continuity, and that their interpretation of the apostolic purpose with respect to worship is the interpretation that has been generally received in Christendom as far back as we can go.

II.

VICISSITUDES

CERTAIN of the necromancers of the far East are said to have the power of causing a tree to spring up, spread its branches, blossom, and bear fruit before the eyes of the lookers-on within the space of a few moments.

Modern liturgies have sometimes been brought into being by a process as extemporaneous as this, but not such was the genesis of the Book of Common Prayer.

There are at least eight forms under which the Prayer Book has been from time to time authoritatively set forth—five English, one Scottish, one Irish, and one American; so that, if we would be accurate, we are bound to specify, when we speak of "The Prayer Book," which of several Prayer Books we have in mind.

The truth is, there exists in connection with everything that grows, whether it be plant, animal, or building, a certain mystery like that which attaches to what, in the case of a man, we call personal identity. Which is the true, the actual Napoleon? Is it the Napoleon of the Directory, or the Napoleon of the Consulate, or the Napoleon of the Empire? At each epoch we discern a different phase of the man's character, and yet we are compelled to acknowledge, in the face of all the variations, that we have to do with one and the same man.

But just as a ship acquires, as we may say, her personal identity when she is launched and named, even though there may be a great deal yet to be done in the way of finishing and furnishing before she can be pronounced seaworthy, so it is with a book that is destined to undergo repeated revision and reconstruction, it does acquire, on the day when it is first published, and first given a distinctive title, a certain character the losing of which would be the loss of personal identity. There is many an old cathedral that might properly enough be called a re-edited book in stone. Norman architecture, Early English, Decorated, and Perpendicular, all are there, and yet one dominant thought pervades the building. Notwithstanding the many times it has been retouched, the fabric still expresses to the eye the original creative purpose of the designer; there is no possibility of our mistaking Salisbury for York or Peterborough for London.

The first Book of Common Prayer was built up of blocks that for the most part had been previously used in other buildings, but the resulting structure exhibited, from the very moment it received a name, such distinct and unmistakable characteristics as have guaranteed it personal identity through more than three hundred years. Hence, while it is in one sense true that there are no fewer than eight Books of Common Prayer, it is in another sense equally true that the Book of Common Prayer is one.

An identity of purpose, of scope, and of spirit shows itself in all its various forms under which the book exists, so that whether we are speaking of the First Prayer Book of King Edward the Sixth, or of the book adopted by the Church of Ireland after its disestablishment, or of the American Book of Common Prayer, what we have in mind is, in a very real and deep sense, one and the same thing.

Let us proceed now to a rapid survey of the facts connected with the first issue of the Common Prayer.

For a period long anterior to the Reformation there had been in use among the English brief books of devotion known as "primers," written in the language of the people. The fact that the public services of the Church were invariably conducted in the Latin tongue made a resort to such expedients as this necessary, unless religion was to be reserved as the private property of ecclesiastics.

By a curious process of evolution the primer, from having been in mediæval times a book wholly religious and devotional, has come to be in our day a book wholly secular and educational. We associate it with Noah Webster and the Harper Brothers. The New England Primer of the Puritans, with its odd jumble of piety and the three R's, marks a point of transition from the ancient to the modern type.

But this by the way. The primer we are now concerned with is the devotional primer of the times just previous to the Reformation. This, as a rule, contained prayers, the Belief, the Ave Maria, a litany of some sort, the Ten Commandments, and whatever else there might be that in the mind of the compiler came under the head of "things which a Christian ought to know." There were three of these primers set forth during the reign of Henry the Eighth, one in 1535, one in 1539, and one in 1545. During the space that intervened between the publication of the second and that of the third of these primers, appeared "The Litany and Suffrages," a formulary compiled, as is generally believed, by Cranmer, the then Archbishop of Canterbury, and in substance identical with the Litany we use to-day. This Litany of 1544 has been properly described as "the precursor and first instalment of the English Book of Common Prayer." It was the nucleus or centre of crystallization about which the other constituent portions of our manual of worship were destined to be grouped. A quaint exhortation was prefixed to this Litany, in which it was said to have been set forth "because the not understanding the prayers and suffrages formerly used caused that the people came but slackly to the processions." Besides the primers and the Litany, there were printed in Henry's reign various editions of a book of Epistles and Gospels in English. There was also published a Psalter in Latin and English.

All this looked rather to the edification of individual Christians in their private devotional life than to the public worship of the Church, but we are not to suppose that meanwhile the larger interests of the whole body were forgotten. So early as in the year 1542, Convocation, which according to the Anglican theory stands toward the Church in the same attitude that Parliament holds to the State, appointed a Committee of Eight to review and correct the existing service-books. We know very little as to the proceedings of this committee, but that something was done, and a real impulse given to liturgical revision, is evidenced by the fact that at a meeting of Convocation held soon after King Henry's death a resolution prevailed "That the books of the Bishops and others who by the command of the Convocation have labored in examining, reforming, and publishing the divine service, may be produced and laid before the examination of this house."

The next important step in the process we are studying was the publication by authority in the early spring of 1548, of an Order of the Communion, as it was called, a formulary prepared by Cranmer to enable the priest, after having consecrated the elements in the usual manner, to distribute them to the people with the sentences of delivery spoken in English. The priest, that is to say, was to proceed with the service of the Mass as usual in the Latin tongue, but after he had himself received the bread and the wine, he was to proceed to a service of Communion for the people in a speech they could understand.

Almost everything in this tentative document, as we may call it, was subsequently incorporated in the Office of the Holy Communion as we are using it to-day.

We have, then, as an abiding result of the liturgical experiments made in anticipation of the actual setting forth of an authoritative Prayer Book, the Litany and this Order of the Communion.

The time was now ripe for something better and more complete; a new king was upon the throne, and one whose counsellors were better disposed toward change than ever Henry had been. The great movement we know under the name of the Reformation touched the life of the Christian Church in every one of its three great departments—doctrine, discipline, and worship. In Henry's mind, however, the question appears to have been almost exclusively one of discipline or polity. His quarrel was not with the accepted theological errors of his day, for as Defender of the Faith he covered some of the worst of them with his shield. Neither was he ill-disposed toward the methods and usages of public worship so far as we can judge. His quarrel first, last, and always was with a certain rival claimant of power, whose pretended authority he was determined to drive out of the realm, to wit, the Pope. But while it was thus with Henry, it was far otherwise with many of the more thoughtful and devout among his theologians, and when the restraint that had been laid on them was removed by the king's death, they welcomed the opportunity to apply to doctrine and worship the same reforming touch that had already remoulded polity.

An enlarged Committee of Convocation sat at Windsor in the summer of 1548, and as a result there was finally set forth, and ordered to be put into use on Whitsunday, 1549, what has become known in history as the "First Prayer Book of Edward VI."

To dwell on those features of the First Book that have remained unaltered to the present day would be superfluous; I shall therefore, in speaking of it, confine myself to the distinctive and characteristic points in which it differs from the Prayer Books that have succeeded it.

It is worthy of note that in the title page of the First Book there is a clear distinction drawn between the Church Universal, or what we call in the *Te Deum* "the holy Church throughout all the world," and that particular Church to which King Edward's subjects, in virtue of their being Englishmen, belonged. The book is said to be "the Book of the Common Prayer and administration of the Sacraments and other Rites and Ceremonies of THE CHURCH, after the use of the Church of England." "THE CHURCH" is recognized as being a larger and, perhaps, older thing than the CHURCH OF ENGLAND, while at the same time it is intimated that only through such *use* of these same prayers and sacraments as the English Church ordains and authorizes can English folk come into communion with the great family of believers spread over the whole earth.

The Preface is a singularly racy piece of English, in which with the utmost plainness of speech the compilers give their reasons for having dealt with the old services as they have done. This reappears in the English Prayer Book of the present day under the title "Concerning the Service of the Church," and so described is placed after the Preface written in 1662 by the Revisers of the Restoration.

The Order for Daily Morning Prayer, as we name it, is called in Edward's First Book "An Order for Matins daily through the year." Similarly, what we call the Order for Daily Evening Prayer was styled "An Order for Evensong." These beautiful names, "Matins" and "Evensong," which it is a great pity to have lost, for surely there is nothing superstitious about them, disappeared from the book as subsequently revised, and save in the Lectionary of the Church of England have no present recognition. One of them, however, Evensong, seems to be coming very generally into colloquial use. The Order for Matins began with the Lord's Prayer. Then, after the familiar versicles still in use, including two that have no place in our American book, "O God, make speed to save me. O Lord, make haste to help me," there followed in full the 95th Psalm, a portion of which is known to us as the *Venite*. From this point the service proceeded, as in the English Prayer Book of to-day, through the Collect for Grace, where it came to an end. The structure of Evensong was similar, beginning with the Lord's Prayer and ending, as our shortened Evening Prayer now does, with the Collect for Aid against Perils. Then followed the Athanasian Creed, and immediately afterward came the Introits, Collects, Epistles, and Gospels.

These Introits, so-called, were psalms appointed to be sung when the priest was about to begin the Holy Communion. They had been an ancient feature of divine service, but were dropped from the subsequent books as a required feature of the Church's worship.

The title of the Communion Service in Edward's First Book is as follows : "The Supper of the Lord and the Holy Communion commonly called the Mass." Immediately after the Prayer for Purity—*i. e*, in the place where we have the Ten Commandments, comes the *Gloria in Excelsis*. The service then proceeds very much as with us, except that the Prayer for the Church Militant and the Consecration Prayer are welded into one, and the Prayer of Humble Access given a place immediately before the reception of the elements. I note, in passing, certain phrases and sentences that are peculiar to the Communion Office of the First Book, as, for instance, this from the Prayer for the whole state of Christ's Church : "And here we do give unto thee most high praise and hearty thanks for the wonderful grace and virtue declared in all thy saints from the beginning of the world, and chiefly in the most glorious and blessed Virgin Mary, Mother of thy Son Jesus Christ our Lord and God, and in the holy patriarchs, prophets, apostles, and martyrs, whose examples, O Lord, and steadfastness in thy faith and keeping thy holy commandments grant us to follow. We commend unto thy mercy, O Lord, all other thy servants which are departed hence from us with the sign of faith and do now rest in the sleep of peace. Grant unto them, we beseech thee, thy mercy and everlasting peace, and that at the day of the general resurrection we and all they which be of the mystical body of thy Son may altogether be set on his right hand."

And this from the closing portion of the Consecration: "Yet we beseech thee to accept this our bounden duty and service, and command these our prayers and supplications by the ministry of thy holy angels to be brought up into thy holy tabernacle before the sight of thy divine majesty."

Following close upon the Communion Service came the Litany, differing very little from what we have to-day, save in the memorable petition, "From the tyranny of the Bishop of Rome and all his detestable enormities, good Lord deliver us."

The Baptismal Offices of the First Book contain certain unique features. The sign of the cross is ordered to be made on the child's breast as well as on his forehead. There is a form of exorcism said over the infant in which the unclean spirit is commanded to come out and to depart. There is also the giving of the "Crisome" or white vesture as a symbol of innocence. "Take this white vesture for a token of the innocency which by God's grace in this holy sacrament of Baptism is given unto thee, and for a sign whereby thou art admonished, so long as thou livest, to give thyself to innocency of living, that after this transitory life thou mayest be partaker of the life everlasting."

The Catechism in Edward VI. First Book, as in the subsequent books down to 1662, is made a part of the Confirmation Office, although it does not clearly appear that the children were expected to say it as a preliminary to the service.

The Office for the Visitation of the Sick contains provision for private confession and absolution, and also directs that the priest shall anoint the sick man with oil if he be desired to do so.

The Office for the Communion of the Sick allows the practice of what is called the reservation of the elements, but contains also, be it observed, that rubric which has held its place through all the changes the Prayer Book has undergone, where we are taught that if the sick man by any "just impediment fail to receive the sacrament of Christ's body and blood, the curate shall instruct him that if he do truly repent him of his sins and steadfastly believe that Jesus Christ hath suffered death upon the cross for him . . . he doth eat and drink the body and blood of our Saviour Christ, profitably to his soul's health although he do not receive the sacrament with his mouth."

The Burial Office contains a recognition of prayer for the dead, but except in the matter of the arrangement of the parts differs but little from the service still in use. A special Introit, Collect, Epistle, and Gospel are appointed "for the Celebration of the Holy Communion when there is a Burial of the Dead."

A Commination Office for Ash-Wednesday, substantially identical with that still in use in the Church of England, concludes the book.

The First Prayer Book of King Edward the Sixth, memorable as it was destined to become, proved, so far as actual use was concerned, but short-lived. It became operative, as we have seen, on Whitsunday, 1549, but it was soon evident that while the new services went too far in the direction of reform to please the friends of the ancient order of things, they did not go far enough to meet the wishes of the reforming party.

Before the year was out no fewer than three translations of the Liturgy into Latin had been undertaken with a view to informing the Protestant divines of the Continent as to what their English colleagues were doing. "There was already within the Church" (of England), writes Cardwell, in his comparison of Edward's two books, "a party, though probably not numerous, which espoused the peculiar sentiments of Calvin; there were others, and Cranmer, it appears, had recently been one of them, adhering strictly to the opinions of Luther; there were many, and those among the most active and the most learned, who adopted the views of Bullinger and the theologians of Zurich; there was a still larger body anxious to combine all classes of Protestants under one general confession, and all these, though with distinct objects and different degrees of impatience, looked forward to a revision of the Liturgy, to bring it more completely into accordance with their own sentiments."

As a result of the agitation thus vividly pictured by Cardwell, there came forth in 1552 the book known as the Second Prayer Book of King Edward VI., a work of the very greatest interest, for the reason that it was destined to become the basis of all future revisions. Whitsunday, 1549, was the day when the First Book began to be used. The Feast of All Saints, 1552, was the date officially appointed for the introduction of the Second Book. Presently King Edward died, and by an act of Mary passed in October, 1553, the use of his Book became illegal on and after December 20th of that year. It thus appears that the First Book was in use for two years and about four months, and the Second Book one year and about two months. A memorable three years and a half for the English-speaking peoples of all time to come, for it is not too much to say that while the language of Tyndale and of Cranmer continues to be heard on earth, the devotions then put into form will keep on moulding the religious thought and firing the spiritual imagination of this race.

The points in which the second of King Edward's two books differs from the first are of such serious moment and the general complexion of the later work has in it such an access of Protestant coloring, that high Anglican writers have been in the habit of attributing the main features of the revision to the interference of the Continental Reformers. "If it had not been for the impertinent meddling," they have been accustomed to say, "of such foreigners as Bucer, Peter Martyr, and John a-Lasco, we might have been enjoying at the present day the admirable and truly Catholic devotions set forth in the fresh morning of the Reformation, before the earth-born vapors of theological controversy and ecclesiastical partisanship had beclouded an otherwise fair sky." But it does not appear that there is any solid foundation in fact for these complaints.

The natural spread of the spirit of reform among the people of the realm, taken in connection with the changes of opinion which the swift movement of the times necessarily engendered in the minds of the leading divines, are of themselves quite sufficient to account for what took place. Certainly, if the English of that day were at all like their descendants in our time, it is in the highest degree unlikely that they would have allowed a handful of learned refugees to force upon them changes which their own sober judgment did not approve.

The truth is, very little is certainly known as to the details of what was done in the making of Edward's Second Book. Even the names of the members of the committee intrusted with the revision are matter of conjecture, and of the proceedings of that body no authentic record survives. What we do possess and are in a position to criticise is the book itself, and to a brief review of the points in which it differs from its predecessor we will now pass.

Upon taking up the Second Book after laying down the First, one is struck immediately with the changed look of Morning Prayer. This is no longer called Matins, and no longer begins as before with the Lord's Prayer. An Introduction has been prefixed to the office consisting of a collection of sentences from Holy Scripture, all of them of a penitential character, and besides these of an Exhortation, a Confession, and an Absolution. There can be little doubt that this opportunity for making public acknowledgment of sin and hearing the declaration of God's willingness to forgive, was meant to counterbalance the removal from the book of all reference, save in one instance, to private confession and absolution. The Church of England has always retained in her Visitation Office a permission to the priest to pronounce absolution privately to the sick man. This was a feature of the First Book that was not disturbed in the Second. But wherever else they found anything that seemed to look toward the continuance of the system familiarly known to us under the name of "the Confessional," they expunged it. Between the Exhortation and the Confession there is, in point of literary merit, a noticeable contrast, and it is scarcely to be believed that both formularies can have proceeded from one and the same pen. Another step in the Protestant direction was the prohibition of certain vestments that in the First Book had been allowed, as the alb and cope. The Introit Psalms were taken away. The word "table" was everywhere substituted for the word "altar." The changes in the Office of the Holy Communion were numerous and significant. The Ten Commandments, for instance, were inserted in the place where we now have them. The *Gloria in Excelsis* was transferred from the beginning of the service to the end. The Exhortations were re-written. The supplication for the dead was taken out of the Prayer for the whole state of Christ's Church, and the words "militant here on earth" were added to the title with a view to confining the scope of the intercession to the circle of people still alive. The Confession, Absolution, Comfortable Words, and Prayer of Humble Access were placed before the Consecration instead of after it. Most important of all was the change of the words appointed to be said in delivering the elements to the communicants. In the First Book these had been, "The body of our Lord Jesus Christ which was given for thee, preserve thy body and soul unto everlasting life," and in the case of the cup, "The blood of our Lord Jesus Christ, which was shed for thee, preserve thy body and soul unto everlasting life." For these were now substituted in the one instance the words, "Take and eat this in remembrance that Christ died for thee, and feed on him in thy heart by faith, with thanksgiving," and in the other, "Drink this in remembrance that Christ's blood was shed for thee, and be thankful."

From the Office for the Communion of the Sick the direction to reserve the elements was omitted, as was also the permission to anoint the sick man with oil. The Service of Baptism was no longer suffered to retain the exorcism of the evil spirit, or the white vesture, or the unction; and there were other items of less important change. Those mentioned reveal plainly enough what was the animus of the revisers. Most evidently the intention was to produce a liturgy more thoroughly reformed, more in harmony with the new tone and temper which the religious thought of the times was taking on.

We come to the Third Book of Common Prayer. Bloody Mary was dead, and Elizabeth had succeeded to the throne.

During the Roman reaction proclamation had been made that all the Reformed service-books should be given up to the ecclesiastical authorities within fifteen days to be burned. This is doubtless the reason why copies of the liturgical books of Edward's reign are now so exceedingly rare. Reprints of them abound, but the originals exist only as costly curiosities.

Soon after Elizabeth's accession a committee of divines

assembled under her authority for the purpose of again revising the formularies.

The queen was personally a High-Churchwoman, and her own judgment is said to have been favorable to taking the first of Edward's two books as the basis of the revision, but a contrary preference swayed the committee, and the lines followed were those of 1552 and not those of 1549.

The new features distinctive of the Prayer Book of Elizabeth, otherwise known as the Prayer Book of 1559, are not numerous. A table of Proper Lessons for Sundays was introduced. The old vestments recognized in the earlier part of King Edward's reign were again legalized. The petition for deliverance from the tyranny of the Pope was struck out of the Litany, and by a compromise peculiarly English in its character, and, as experience has shown, exceedingly well judged, the two forms of words that had been used in the delivery of the elements in the Holy Communion were welded together into the shape in which we have them still.

Queen Elizabeth's Prayer Book continued in use for five-and-forty years. Nothing was more natural than that when she died there should come with the accession of a new dynasty a demand for fresh revision. King James, who was not afflicted with any want of confidence in his own judgment, invited certain representatives of the disaffected party to meet, under his presidency, the Churchmen in council with a view to the settlement of differences. The Puritans had been gaining in strength during Elizabeth's reign, and they felt that they were now in position to demand a larger measure of liturgical reform than that monarch and her advisers had been willing to concede to them.

King James convened his conference at Hampton Court, near London, and he himself was good enough to preside. Very little came of the debate. The Puritans had demanded the discontinuance of the sign of the cross in Baptism, of bowing at the name of Jesus, of the ring in marriage, and of the rite of confirmation. The words "priest" and "absolution" they sought to have expunged from the Prayer Book, and they desired that the wearing of the surplice should be made optional.

Almost nothing was conceded to them. The words "or Remission of Sins" were added to the title of the Absolution, certain Prayers and Thanksgivings were introduced, and that portion of the Catechism which deals with the Sacraments was for the first time set forth. And thus the English Prayer Book started out upon its fourth lease of life destined in this form to endure unchanged, though by no means unassailed, for more than half a century.

A stirring half century it was. The Puritan defeat at Hampton Court was redressed at Naseby. With the coming in of the Long Parliament the Book of Common Prayer went out, and to all appearances the triumph of the Commonwealth meant the final extinction of the usage of liturgical worship on English soil. The book, under its various forms, had lasted just a hundred years when he who

> Nothing common did or mean
> Upon that memorable scene

suffered at Whitehall.

They buried him in St. George's Chapel, Windsor, and no single word of the Prayer Book he had loved and for which he had fought was said over his grave.

On January 3, 1645, Parliament repealed the statutes of Edward VI. and of Elizabeth that had enjoined the use of the Book of Common Prayer, and took order that thereafter only such divine service should be lawful as accorded with what was called the *Directory*, a manual of suggestions with respect to public worship adopted by the Presbyterian party as a substitute for the ancient liturgy.

With the restoration of the Stuarts in 1660 came naturally the restoration of the Prayer Book, and with equal naturalness a revision of it. But of what sort should the revision be, and under whose auspices conducted? This was an anxious question for the advisers, civil and ecclesiastical, of the restored king. Should the second Charles take up the book just as it had fallen from the hands of the first Charles, unchanged in line or letter, or should he seek by judicious alterations and timely concessions to win back for the national Church the good-will and loyalty of those who, eighteen years before, had broken down her hedge? The situation may be described as triangular.

The king's secret and personal sympathies were probably all along with the Roman Church; his official allegiance was plainly due to the Church of England; and yet, at the same time, he owed much to the forbearance of the men who had been dominant under the Commonwealth. The mind of the nation had, indeed, reacted toward monarchy, but not with such an absolute and hardy renunciation of the doctrines of popular sovereignty as to make it safe for the returning king to do precisely as he chose. The glorious Revolution that was destined so soon to follow upon the heels of the gracious Restoration gave evidence, when it came, that there were some things the people of England prized even more highly than an hereditary throne. Misgivings as to the amount there might still be of this sort of electricity in the atmosphere suggested to the king and his counsellors the expediency of holding a conference, at which the leaders on either side might bring forward their strong reasons in favor of this or that method of dealing with the ecclesiastical question in general, and more especially with the vexed problem of worship.

Accordingly, early in the spring of 1661 the King issued a royal warrant summoning to meet at the Savoy Palace in the Strand an equal number of representatives of both parties—namely, one-and-twenty Churchmen and one-and-twenty Presbyterians.

The Episcopal deputation consisted of twelve bishops and nine other divines called coadjutors. The Presbyterians had also their twelve principal men and their nine coadjutors.

Conspicuous among the Episcopalians for weight of learning were Bishops Sanderson, Cosin, and Walton, and Doctors Pearson, Sparrow, and Heylin. Baxter, Reynolds, Calamy, and Lightfoot were the most notable of the Presbyterians.

The conference, which has ever since been known from its place of meeting (an old palace of the Piedmontese Ambassadors) as the Savoy Conference, convened on April 15, 1661. For various reasons, it was evident from the outset that the Churchmen were in a position of great advantage. In the first place, signs and tokens of a renewed confidence in monarchy and of a revived attachment to the reigning House were becoming daily more numerous.

Before he had had a chance to test the strength of the existing political parties and to know how things really stood, Charles had borne himself very discreetly toward the Presbyterians, and had held out hopes to them which, as the event proved, were destined never to be realized. In a declaration put forth in the autumn of 1660, after he had been for some months on English soil, he had even gone so far as to say: " When we were in Holland we were attended by many grave and learned ministers from hence, who were looked upon as the most able and principal asserters of the Presbyterian opinions; with whom we had as much conference as the multitude of affairs which were then upon us would permit us to have, and to our great satisfaction and comfort found them persons full of affection to us, of zeal for the peace of the Church and State, and neither enemies, as they have been given out to be, to episcopacy or liturgy, but modestly to desire such alterations in either, as without shaking foundations might best allay the present distempers "

By the time the conference met it had become evident, from votes taken in Parliament and otherwise, that the Churchmen could sustain toward their opponents a somewhat stiffer attitude than this without imperilling their cause. Another great advantage enjoyed by the Episcopalians grew out of the fact that they were the party in possession. They had only to profess themselves satisfied with the Prayer Book as it stood, in order to throw the Presbyterians into the position of assailants, and defense is always easier than attack. Sheldon, the Bishop of London, was not slow to perceive this. At the very first meeting of the conference, he is reported to have said that "as the Non-conformists, and not the bishops, had sought for the conference, nothing could be done till the former had delivered their exceptions in writing, together with the additional forms and alterations which they desired." Upon which Bishop Burnet in his *History of his own Times* remarks: "Sheldon saw well what the effect would be of putting them to make all their demands at once. The number of them raised a mighty outcry against them, as people that could never be satisfied."

The Presbyterians, however, took up the challenge, set to work at formulating their objections, and appointed Richard Baxter, the most famous of their number, to show what could be done in the way of making a better manual of worship than the Book of Common Prayer.

Baxter, a truly great man and wise in a way, though scarcely in the liturgical way, was guilty of the incredible folly of undertaking to construct a Prayer Book within a fortnight.

Of this liturgy it is probably safe to say that no denomination of Christians, however anti-prelatical or eccentric, would for a moment dream of adopting it, if, indeed, there be a single local congregation anywhere that could be persuaded to employ it. The characteristic of the devotions is lengthiness. The opening sentence of the prayer with which the book begins contains by actual count eighty-three words. It is probable that Baxter by his rash act did more to injure the cause of intelligent and reverential liturgical revision than any ten men have done before or since. In every discussion of the subject he is almost sure to be brought forward as "the awful example."

A document much more to the point than Baxter's Liturgy was the formal catalogue of faults and blemishes alleged against the Prayer Book, which the Puritan members of the conference in due time brought in. This indictment, for it may fairly be called such, since it was drawn up in separate counts, is very interesting reading. Of the "exceptions against the Book of Common Prayer," as the Puritans named their list of liturgical grievances, some must strike almost any reader of the present day as trivial and unworthy. Others again there are that draw a sympathetic *Amen* from many quarters to-day. To an American Episcopalian the catalogue is chiefly interesting as showing how ready and even eager were our colonial ancestors of a hundred years ago to remove out of the way such known rocks of offence as they could. An attentive student of the American Prayer Book cannot fail to be struck with the number of instances in which the text gives evidence of the influence exerted over the minds of our revisers by what had been urged, more than a hundred years before, by the Puritan members of the Savoy Conference. The defeat of 1661 was, in a measure at least, avenged in 1789. It is encouraging to those who cast their bread upon liturgical waters to notice after how many days the return may come. But the conference, to all outward seeming, was a failure.

Baxter's unhappy Prayer Book was its own sufficient refutation, and as for the list of special grievances it was met by the bishops with an "Answer" that was full of hard raps and conceded almost nothing.

A few detached paragraphs may serve to illustrate the general tone of this reply. Here, for instance, is the comment of the bishops upon the request of the Puritans to be allowed occasionally to substitute extemporaneous for liturgical devotions. "The gift or rather spirit of prayer consists in the inward graces of the spirit, not in extempore expressions which any man of natural parts having a voluble tongue and audacity may attain to without any special gift." Nothing very conciliatory in that. To the complaint that the Collects are too short, the bishops reply that they cannot for that reason be accounted faulty, being like those "short but prevalent prayers in Scripture, Lord, be merciful to me a sinner. Lord, increase our faith." The Puritans had objected to the antiphonal element in the Prayer-Book services, and desired to have nothing of a responsive character allowed beyond the single word *Amen*. "But," rejoin the bishops, "they directly practise the contrary in one of their principal parts of worship, singing of psalms, where the people bear as great a part as the minister. If this way be done in Hopkin's why not in David's Psalms; if in metre, why not in prose; if in a psalm, why not in a litany?" Sharp, but not winning.

The Puritans had objected to the people's kneeling while the Commandments were read on the score that ignorant worshippers might mistake the Decalogue for a form of prayer. With some asperity the bishops reply that "why Christian people should not upon their knees ask their pardon for their life forfeited for the breach of every commandment and pray for grace to keep them for the time to come they must be more than 'ignorant' that can scruple."

The time during which the conference at the Savoy should continue its sessions had been limited to four months. This period expired on July 24, 1661, and the apparently fruitless disputation was at an end. Meanwhile, however, Convocation, the recognized legislature of the Church of England, had begun to sit, and the bishops had undertaken a revision of the Prayer Book after their own mind, and with slight regard to what they had been hearing from their critics at the Savoy. The bulk of their work, which included, it is said, more than six hundred alterations, most of them of a verbal character and of no great importance, was accomplished within the compass of a single month. It is consoling to those who within our own memory have been charged with indecent haste for seeking to effect a revision of the American Book of Common Prayer within a period of nine years, to find this precedent in ecclesiastical history for their so great rashness.

Since Charles the Second's day there has been no formal revision of the Prayer Book of the Church of England by the Church of England.

Some slight relaxations of liturgical use on Sundays have been made legal by Act of Parliament, but in all important respects the Prayer Book of Victoria is identical with the book set forth by Convocation and sanctioned by Parliament shortly after the collapse of the Savoy Conference. Under no previous lease of life did the book enjoy anything like so long a period of continued existence. Elizabeth's book was the longest lived of all that preceded the Restoration, but that only continued in use five-and-forty years. But the Prayer Book of 1661 has now held its own in England for two centuries and a quarter. When, therefore, we are asked to accept the first Edwardian Book as the only just exponent of the religious mind of England, it is open to us to reply, "Why should we, seeing that the Caroline Book has served as the vehicle of English devotion for a period seventy-five times as long?" The most voluminous of the additions made to the Prayer Book, in 1661, were the Office for the Baptism of Adults and the Forms of Prayer to be used at Sea. The wide diffusion, under the Commonwealth, of what were then called Anabaptist opinions, had brought it to pass that throughout the kingdom there were thousands of men and women who had grown up unbaptized. At the time of the Reformation such a thing as an unchristened Christendom seems not to have been thought possible. At any rate no provision was made for the contingency. But upon the spread of liberty of religious thought there followed, logically enough, the spread of liberty of religious action, and it was not strange that after a whole generation had spent its life in controversy of the warmest sort over this very point of Baptism, there were found to be in England multitudes of the unbaptized.

Another reason assigned in the Preface of the English Prayer Book for the addition of this office was that it might be used for the baptizing of "natives in the plantations and other converts." This is the first hint of any awakening of the conscience of the English

Church to a sense of duty toward those strangers and foreigners who in the "Greater Britain" of these later days fill so large a place. The composition of the office, which differs very little, perhaps scarcely enough, from that appointed for the Baptism of Infants, is attributed to Griffith, the Bishop of St. Asaph. The compiler of the Forms of Prayer to be used at Sea was Bishop Sanderson, famous among English theologians as an authority on casuistry. He must have found it rather a nice case of conscience to decide whether a Stuart divine in preparing forms of prayer for a navy that had been the creation of Oliver Cromwell ought wholly to omit an acknowledgment of the nation's obligation to that stout-hearted, if non-Episcopal Christian. Other additions of importance made at this revision were the General Thanksgiving, in all probability the work of Reynolds, a conforming Presbyterian divine, the Collect, Epistle, and Gospel for the Sixth Sunday after the Epiphany, the Prayer for Parliament, upon the lines of which our own Prayer for Congress was afterward modelled, and the Prayer for All Sorts and Conditions of Men. In the Litany the words "rebellion" and "schism" were introduced into one of the suffrages, becoming tide-marks of the havoc wrought in Church and State by what the revisers, doubtless, looked back upon as "the flood of the ungodly." The words "Bishops, Priests, and Deacons" were substituted for "Bishops, Pastors, and Ministers of the Church." New Collects were appointed for the Third Sunday in Advent and for St. Stephen's Day. Both of these are distinct gains, albeit had the opinion then prevailed that to introduce into the Prayer Book anything from the pen of a living writer is an impiety, we should have gained neither of them.

Another important change made in 1662 was the adoption for the Sentences, Epistles and Gospels of the language of King James's Bible in place of that of earlier versions. This principle was not applied to the Psalter, to the Decalogue, or, in fact, to any of the portions of Scripture contained in the Communion Service.

It is also interesting to note that the Confession in the Holy Communion, which the earlier rubric had directed should be said by one of the congregation, or else by one of the ministers, or by the priest himself, " was now made general and enjoined upon all the worshippers."

Most suggestive of all, however, was the reinsertion at the end of the Communion Service of a certain Declaration about the significance of the act of kneeling at the reception of the elements, which had, as some say, irregularly and without proper authority, found its way into the Second Book of Edward VI., but had been omitted from all subsequent books till now. This Declaration, which from its not being printed in red ink is known to those who dislike it under the name of "the black rubric," was undoubtedly intended to ease the consciences of those who scrupled to kneel at the altar-rail for fear of seeming to countenance that superstitious adoration of the elements known to and stigmatized by the Reformers as "host-worship." The language of the black rubric as it stood in Edward's Second Book was as follows: "Although no order can be so perfectly devised but it may be of some, either for their ignorance and infirmity, or else of malice and obstinacy, misconstrued, depraved, and interpreted in a wrong part; and yet because brotherly charity willeth that so much as conveniently may be offences should be taken away; therefore we willing to do the same: whereas, it is ordained in the Book of Common Prayer, in the Administration of the Lord's Supper, that the communicants kneeling should receive the Holy Communion, which thing being well meant for a signification of the humble and grateful acknowledging of the benefits of Christ given unto the worthy receiver, and to avoid the profanation and disorder, which about the Holy Communion might else ensue, lest yet the same kneeling might be thought or taken otherwise; we do declare that it is not meant thereby, that any adoration is done or ought to be done, either unto the sacramental bread or wine there bodily received or unto any real and essential presence there being of Christ's natural flesh and blood. For as concerning the sacramental bread and wine they remain still in their very natural substances, and therefore may not be adored, for that were idolatry to be abhorred of all faithful Christians: and as concerning the natural body and blood of our Saviour Christ, they are in heaven and not here, for it is against the truth of Christ's true natural body to be in more places than in one at one time."

In restoring this significant Declaration, the revisers of 1662 substituted the words "corporal presence" for the words "real and substantial presence," but probably with no intention other than that of making the original meaning more plain. The fact that in the teeth and eyes of the black rubric the practice known as Eucharistical adoration has become widely prevalent in the

Church of England, only shows how little dependence can be placed on forms of words to keep even excellent and religious people from doing the things they have a mind to do.

In taking leave of the Caroline revision, it may be permitted to dwell for a moment upon the serious character of the conclusion reached by the ecclesiastical leaders of that day. An opportunity was given them to conciliate dissent. Without going all lengths, without in any measure imperilling the great foundation principles of Anglican religion, they might, it would seem, have won back to the national church thousands of those whom their sternness not only repelled but permanently embittered. But it was the hour of victory with the Churchmen, and "Woe to the conquered" seems to have been their cry. They set their faces as a flint against concession; they passed their iron-clad act of uniformity, and now for more than two hundred years religion in Great Britain has been a household divided against itself. Perhaps nothing that the men of the Restoration could have done would have made it otherwise. Perhaps the familiar question of the cynical Dean of St. Patrick's, "What imports it how large a gate you open, if there be always left a number who place a pride and a merit in refusing to enter?" was a fair question, and fatal to any dream of unity. And yet one may be pardoned for believing that had a little of the oil of brotherly kindness been poured upon those troubled waters we whom the waves still buffet might to-day be sailing a smoother sea.

As stated above, the Convocation of 1662 gave to the Prayer Book of the Church of England the form it has ever since retained. But it must not be supposed that no efforts have been made meanwhile to bring changes to pass. The books written upon the subject form a literature by themselves.

The one really serious attempt to reconstruct the Liturgy in post-Caroline times was that which grew naturally enough out of the Revolution of 1688. In every previous crisis of political change, the Prayer Book had felt the tremor along with the statute-book.

Church and State, like heart and brain, are sympathetically responsive to one another; revisions of rubrics go naturally along with revisions of codes. It was only what might have been anticipated, therefore, that when William and Mary came to the throne a Commission should issue for a new review. If Elizabeth had found it necessary to revise the book, if James had found it necessary, if Charles had found it necessary, why should not the strong hand of William of Orange be laid upon the pages? But this time the rule was destined to find its exception. The work of review was, indeed, undertaken by a Royal Commission, including among its members the great names of Stillingfleet, Tillotson, and Beveridge, but nothing came of their work. Convocation again showed itself unfriendly to anything like concessive measures, and so complete was the obscurity into which the doings of the Commission fell, that even as late as 1849, Cardwell, in the third edition of his *History of Conferences*, speaks as if he knew nothing of the whereabouts of the record. In 1854 the manuscript minutes of the Commission's proceedings were discovered in the Library of Lambeth Palace, and by order of Parliament printed as a Blue-book. The same document has also been published in a more readable form by Bagster. One rises from the perusal of this Broad Church Prayer Book—for such, perhaps, Tillotson's attempt may not unfairly be called—profoundly thankful that the promoters of it were not suffered to succeed. The Preface to our American Book of Common Prayer refers to this attempted review of 1689 "as a great and good work." But the greatness and the goodness must have lain in the motive, for one fails to discern them either in the matter or in the manner of what was recommended.

Even Macaulay, Whig that he is, fails not to put on record his condemnation of the literary violence which the Prayer Book so narrowly escaped at the hands of the Royal Commission of 1689. Terseness was not the special excellency of Macaulay's own style, yet even he resented Bishop Patrick's notion that the Collects could be improved by amplification. One of the few really good suggestions made by the Commissioners was that of using the Beatitudes in the Office of the Holy Communion as an alternate for the Decalogue. There are certain festivals of the Christian year when such a substitution would be most timely and refreshing.

We make a leap now of just a hundred years. From 1689 we pass to 1789, and find ourselves in the city of Philadelphia, at a convention assembled for the purpose of framing a constitution and setting forth a liturgy for a body of Christians destined to be known as the Protestant Episcopal Church in the United States of America. During the interval between the issue of the Declaration of Independence and the Ratification of the Constitution of the United States, the people in this country who had been brought up in the communion of the Church of England found themselves ecclesiastically in a very delicate position indeed. As colonists they had been canonically under the spiritual jurisdiction of the Bishop of London, a somewhat remote diocesan. But with this Episcopal bond broken and no new one formed, they seemed to be in a peculiar sense adrift. It does not fall to me to narrate the steps that led to the final establishment of the episcopacy upon a sure foundation, nor yet to trace the process through which the Church's legislative system came gradually to its completion. Our interest is a liturgical one, and our subject matter the evolution of the Prayer Book. I say nothing, therefore, of other matters that were debated in the Convention of 1789, but shall propose instead that we confine ourselves to what was said and done about the Prayer Book. In order, however, fully to appreciate the situation we must go back a little. In a half-formal and half-informal fashion there had come into existence, four years before this Convention of 1789 assembled, an American Liturgy now known by the name of *The Proposed Book*. It had been compiled on the basis of the English Prayer Book by a Committee of three eminent clergymen, Dr. White of Pennsylvania, Dr. William Smith of Maryland, and Dr. Wharton of Delaware. Precisely what measure of acceptance this book enjoyed, or to what extent it came actually into use, are difficult, perhaps hopeless questions.

What we know for certain is that the public opinion of the greater number of Churchmen rejected it as inadequate and unsatisfactory. In the Convention of

1789 *The Proposed Book* does not seem to have been seriously considered in open debate at all, though doubtless there was much talk about it, much controversy over its merits and demerits at Philadelphia dinner-tables and elsewhere while the session was in progress.

The truth is, the changes set forth in *The Proposed Book* were too sweeping to commend themselves to the sober second-thought of men whose blood still showed the tincture of English conservatism. Possibly also some old flames of Tory resentment were rekindled, here and there, by the prominence given in the book to a form of public thanksgiving for the Fourth of July. There were Churchmen doubtless at that day who failed duly to appreciate what were called in the title of the office, "the inestimable blessings of Religious and Civil Liberty." Others again may have been offended by the treatment measured out to the Psalter, which was portioned into thirty selections of two parts each, with the *Benedicite* added at the end, to be used, if desired, on the thirty-first day of any month. Another somewhat crude and unliturgical device was the running together without break of the Morning Prayer and the Litany.

I speak of blemishes, but *The Proposed Book* had its excellences also. Just at present it is the fashion in Anglican circles to heap ridicule and contempt on *The Proposed Book* out of all proportion to its real demerits. Somehow it is thought to compromise us with the English by showing up our ecclesiastical ancestors in an unfavorable light as unlearned and ignorant men. It is treated as people will sometimes treat an old family portrait of a forebear, who in his day was under a cloud, mismanaged trust funds, or made money in the slave trade. Thus a grave historiographer by way of speaking comfortably on this score, assures us that the volume "speedily sunk into obscurity," becoming one of the rarest of the books illustrative of our ecclesiastical annals.

And yet, curiously enough, *The Proposed Book* was in some points more "churchly," using the word in a sense expressive of liturgical accuracy, than the book finally adopted. In the Morning Prayer it has the *Venite* in full and not abridged. The *Benedictus* it also gives entire. A single form of Absolution is supplied. The versicles following upon the Creed are more numerous than ours. In the Evening Prayer the great Gospel Hymns, the *Magnificat* and the *Nunc dimittis*, stand in the places to which we with tardy justice have only just restored them.

Again, if we consider those features of *The Proposed Book* that were retained and made part of the Liturgy in 1789, we shall have further reason to refrain from wholesale condemnation of this tentative work. For example, we owe the two opening sentences of Morning Prayer, "The Lord is in his holy temple" and "From the rising of the sun," to *The Proposed Book*, and also the special form for Thanksgiving Day. And yet, on the whole, the Convention of 1789 acted most wisely in determining that it would make the Prayer Book of the Church of England, rather than *The Proposed Book*, the real basis of revision. It did so, and as a result we have what has served us so well during the first century of our national life—the *Book of Common Prayer and*

Administration of the Sacraments and other rites and ceremonies of the Church according to the use of the Protestant Episcopal Church in the United States of America. The points wherein the American Prayer Book differs from the Prayer Book of the Church of England are too numerous to be catalogued in full. "They will appear," says the Preface (a composition borrowed, by the way, almost wholly from *The Proposed Book*), "and, it is to be hoped, the reasons of them also, upon a comparison of this with the Book of Common Prayer of the Church of England.

The most important differences are the following: The permissive use of "Selections of Psalms in place of the Psalms appointed for the day of the month." This was doubtless suggested by the wholesale transformation of the Psalter in *The Proposed Book* into a series of selections.

The permitted shortening of the Litany is an American feature.

A number of the special prayers, as, for example, the prayer for a sick person, that for persons going to sea, the thanksgivings for a recovery and for a safe return, all these are peculiar to the American use. Extensive alterations were made in the Marriage Service and certain greatly needed ones in the Burial Office. The two most noteworthy differences, however, are the omission from our Prayer Book of the so-called Athanasian Creed, and the insertion in it of that part of the Consecration Prayer in the Communion Office known as the Invocation. The engrafting of this latter feature we owe to the influence of Bishop Seabury, who by this addition not only assimilated the language of our liturgy more closely to that of the ancient formularies of the Oriental Church, but also insured our being kept reminded of the truly spiritual character of Holy Communion. "It is the spirit that quickeneth," this Invocation seems to say; "the flesh profiteth nothing." Quite in line with this was the alteration made at the same time in the language of the Catechism. "The Body and Blood of Christ," says the English Book, "which are verily and indeed taken and received by the faithful in the Lord's Supper."

"The Body and Blood of Christ," says the American Book, "which are spiritually taken and received by the faithful in the Lord's Supper."

Many verbal changes are to be found scattered here and there through the book, some of them for the better, some, perhaps, for the worse. The prevailing purpose seems to have been to expunge all obsolete words and phrases while dealing tenderly with obsolescent ones. In this course, however, the revisers were by no means always and everywhere consistent.

"Prevent," in the sense of "anticipate," is altered in some places but left unchanged in others. In the *Visitation of Prisoners*, an office borrowed from the Irish Prayer Book, the thoroughly obsolete expression, "As you tender," in the sense of "as you value," the salvation of your soul, is retained.

From the Psalter has disappeared in the American Book "Thou tellest my flittings," although why this particular archaism should have been selected for banishment and a hundred others spared, it is not easy to understand.

Perhaps some sudden impatience seized the reviser, like that which moved Bishop Wren, while annotating his Prayer Book, to write on the margin of the calendar for August, "Out with 'dog days' from among the saints."

Considering what a bond of unity the Lord's Prayer appears to be becoming among all English-speaking worshippers, it is, perhaps, to be regretted that our revisers changed the wording of it in two or three places. The excision of "Lighten our darkness" must probably be attributed to the prosaic matter-of-fact temper which had possession of everybody and everything during the last quarter of the eighteenth century.

The Ordinal, the Articles, the Consecration of Churches, and the Institution of Ministers made no part of the Prayer Book as it was set forth in 1789; nor do they, even now, strictly speaking, make a part of it, although in the matter of binding force and legal authority they are on the same footing.

The Ordinal and Articles are substantially identical with the English Ordinal and Articles, save in the matter of a reference to the Athanasian Creed and several references to the connection of Church and State. The Consecration of Churches and the Institution of Ministers are offices distinctively American. If I add that the American Book drops out of the Visitation of the Sick a form of private absolution, and greatly modifies the service for Ash-Wednesday, we shall have made our survey of differences tolerably, though by no means exhaustively complete.

And now what is the lesson taught us by the history of the Prayer Book? Homiletical as the question sounds, it is worth asking.

We have reviewed rapidly, but not carelessly, the

vicissitudes of the book's wonderful career, and we ought to be in a position to draw some sort of instructive inference from it all. Well, one thing taught us is this, the singular power of survival that lives in gracious words. They wondered at the "gracious words which proceeded out of His mouth," and because they wondered at them they treasured them up.

Kind words, says the child's hymn, can never die; neither can kindly words, and kindly in the deepest sense are many, many of the words of the Common Prayer; they touch that which is most catholic in us, that which strongly links us to our kind. There is that in some of the Collects which as it has lasted since the days when Roman emperors were sitting on their thrones, so will it last while man continues what he is, a praying creature.

Another thing taught us by the Prayer Book's history is the duty of being forever on our guard in the religious life against "the falsehood of extremes."

The emancipated thinkers who account all standards of belief to be no better than dungeon walls, scoff at this feature of the Anglican character with much bitterness. "Your Church is a Church of compromises," they say, "and your boasted *Via media* only a coward's path, the poor refuge of the man who dares not walk in the open." But when we see this Prayer Book condemned for being what it is by Bloody Mary, and then again condemned for being what it is by the Long Parliament, the thought occurs to us that possibly there is enshrined in this much-persecuted volume a truth larger than the Romanist is willing to tolerate, or the Puritan generous enough to apprehend.

A third important lesson is that we are not to confound revision with ruin, or to suppose that because a book is marvellously good it cannot conceivably be bettered. Each accomplished revision of the Book of Common Prayer has been a distinct step in advance. If God in his wise providence suffered an excellent growth of devotion to spring up out of the soil of England in the days of Edward the Sixth, and, after many years, determined that like a vine out of Egypt it should be brought across the sea and given root on these shores, we need not fear that we are about to lose utterly our pleasant plant if we notice that the twigs and leaves are adapting themselves to the climate and the atmosphere of the new dwelling-place. The life within the vine remains what it always was. The growth means health. The power of adaptation is the guarantee of a perpetual youth.

REVISION OF THE AMERICAN COMMON PRAYER.

REVISION OF THE AMERICAN COMMON PRAYER.*

THE revision of long established formularies of public worship is, as it ought to be, a matter compassed about with obstacles many and great. A wise doubtfulness prompts conservative minds to throw every mover for change upon the defensive, when liturgical interests are at stake. So many men are born into the world with a native disposition to tamper with and tinker all settled things, and so many more become persuaded, as time goes on, of a personal "mission" to pull down and remake whatever has been once built up, esteeming life a failure unless they have contrived to build each his own monument upon a clearing, that lovers of the old ways are sometimes compelled in sheer self-defence to put on the appearance of being more obstinately set against change than they really are. It ought not to be absolutely impossible to alter a national hand-book of worship (which is what any manual calling itself a Common Prayer must aspire to become), but it is well that it should be all but impossible to do so. Logically it might seem as if the possession of a power to make involved a continuance of power to remake; and so it does, to a certain extent, but only to a certain extent. Living organisms cannot be remodelled with the same freedom as dead matter. A solemnity hangs about the

* First printed in the *American Church Review*, April, 1881.

moment of birth that attaches to no other crisis in a man's life until death comes. Similarly there are certain features which the founders of institutions, the first makers of organic law, imprint lastingly upon their work. We may destroy the living thing so brought to birth; to kill is always possible; but only by very gradual and plastic methods can we hope in any measure to reconstruct the actual embodiment of life once achieved. The men of 1789 had us in their power, even as the men of 1549 had had both them and us. In every creative epoch many things are settled by which unborn generations will be bound.*

It may be urged that this is an argument against adopting liturgies in the first instance as vehicles of worship; and such undoubtedly it is in so far forth as immobility ought in such matters to be reckoned a disadvantage. But we are bound to take into account the gain which comes with immobility as well as the drawbacks. We must consider how large a proportion of the reverence which the great institutes of human life exact from us is due to the fixity of the things themselves. Mont Blanc loses nothing of its hold upon our admiration because we always find it in the same place

---

* Much confusion of thought and speech in connection with our ecclesiastical legislation grows out of not keeping in mind the fact that here in America the organic genetic law of the Church, as well as of the State, is in writing, and compacted into definite propositions. We draw, that is to say, a far sharper distinction than it is possible to do in England between what is constitutional and what is simply statutory. There is no function of our General Convention that answers to the "omnipotence of Parliament." This creative faculty was vacated once for all at the adoption of the Constitution.

Men like to feel that there is something in the world stronger than the individual will, stronger simply because it expresses the settled common-sense of many as to what is fitting and right in contrast with the whim of one. Lawyers, as a class, are almost as conservative as ecclesiastics, and for the very reason that they also are charged with the custody of established forms which it is.important that men should reverence. Laws affecting the tenure of property, the binding force of contracts, the stability of the marriage relation, not only cannot be lightly altered, the very phraseology in which they are couched must be carefully handled, for fear lest with the passing away of the form something of the substance go also.

Moreover, the affections of men fasten themselves very tenaciously to such a trellis as a liturgy affords. The love for "the old words and the old tunes" against which all innovators in hymnody, however deserving, have to do battle, asserts itself under the form of love for the old prayers with ten-fold vehemence. An immense fund of latent heat smoulders beneath the maxim, "Let the ancient customs prevail"; and few of the victories achieved by the papacy are so startling as those that have resulted in the displacement of the liturgical uses of local Churches, that of Paris, for example, by the Roman rite.

But true principles, as we are often reminded, become falsehoods when shoved across the line of proper measure. The very cycles of the astronomers have an end, and the clock-work of the most ancient heavens, or at least our reading of it, calls, from time to time, for readjustment. So long as man continues fallible his best intended workmanship will occasionally demand such alteration for the better as, within the limits already pointed out, may be possible.

Many signs of the times suggest that the hour for a fresh review of the Anglican formularies of worship is nigh at hand. Some of these tokens are written on a sky broad enough to cover the whole English-speaking race, others of them are visible chiefly within our own national horizon. With respect to the English book, Cardwell* writing in 1840 and Freeman † in 1855, considered revision, however desirable in the abstract, to be a thing utterly out of reach, not within the circle, as the parliamentary phrase now runs, of "practical politics."

But it may be fairly questioned whether these high authorities, were they living to-day, would not concur in the judgment of a more recent writer when he says— in language which, *mutatis mutandis*, applies to our own case · "The most weighty plea in favor of timely inquiry into the subject is that the process of revision is actually going on piecemeal, and with no very intelligent survey of the bearings as a preliminary to any one instalment. The New Lectionary of 1871, the Shortened Services Act, the debates in the Convocation of Canterbury on rubrical amendments, none of them marked by any sufficient care or knowledge, and all fraught with at least the possibility of serious consequence, are examples of formal and recognized inroads on the Act of Uniformity; while such practical though unauthorized additions to the scanty group of Anglican

---

* *Conferences*, p. 461.
† *Principles of Divine Service*, vol. i. p. 390.

formularies as the Three Hours' Devotion, Harvest Thanksgivings, Public Institution of Incumbents, Ordination of Readers and Deaconesses, and Children's Services prove incontestably that the narrow limits of the Common Prayer Book are no longer adequate for the spiritual needs of the Church of England. . .

"It is evident, then, that contented acquiescence with the old state of things already belongs to the past, and that a return to it is impossible. We must perforce advance, for good or ill, in the path of revision, and cannot even materially slacken the pace nor defer the crisis. One choice, however, is left in our power, and that is the most important of all, namely, the direction which revision shall take—that of conservative and recuperative addition, or that of further evisceration, ceremonial or devotional."*

A measure looking in the direction towards which this reviewer points was actually passed by the General Convention of our own Church at its late session in October, 1880.

The wording of the Resolution referred to was as follows :

"*Resolved:* That a Joint Committee, to consist of seven bishops, seven presbyters, and seven laymen be appointed to consider and report to the next General Convention whether, in view of the fact that this Church is soon to enter upon the second century of its organized existence in this country, the changed conditions of the national life do not demand certain alterations in the Book of Common Prayer in the direction

* *Church Quarterly Review*, London, October, 1876

of liturgical enrichment and increased flexibility of use." *

In the present article the writer proposes to inquire, in connection with this measure:

(1) What motives may fairly be supposed to have actuated the Convention in allowing so important an initiatory step to be taken?

(2) What measure of authority was conferred on and what scope given to the Joint Committee then constituted?

(3) What reasons exist for considering the present a happy moment to attempt liturgical revision, within certain limits, should such a thing be determined upon?

(4) What serious difficulties and obstacles are likely to be encountered in Committee, in Convention, and in the Church at large?

(5) What particular improvements and adjustments of our existing system would be, in point of fact, best worth the effort necessary to secure them?

I. The interpretation of motives, difficult enough in the case of individuals, becomes mere guess-work when the action under analysis is that of a large body of men. Which one of many considerations urged upon the Convention carried with it the supreme weight of persuasion in this particular instance it is impossible to say. Two or three arguments, however, from their frequent reappearance in the debate may fairly be

* The votes of the House of Bishops are not reported numerically. In the House of Clerical and Lay Deputies the vote stood as follows: "Of the Clergy there were 43 Dioceses represented—Ayes, 33; nays, 9; divided, 1. Of the Laity there were 35 Dioceses represented—Ayes, 20; nays, 11; divided, 4."—*Journal of Convention of* 1880, p. 152.

judged to have exercised a controlling influence. One of these was hinted at in the language of the resolution itself, namely, the call for revision that has grown out of "the changed conditions of the national life." Shrewd and far-seeing as were William White and his coadjutors in their forecast of nineteenth century needs made from the standpoint of the Peace of Versailles, they would have been more than human had they succeeded in anticipating all the civil and ecclesiastical consequences destined to flow from that memorable event. Certainly it ought not to be held strange that this "new America" of ours, with its enormously multiplied territory, its conglomerate of races, its novel forms of association, its multiplicity of industries not dreamed of a generation ago, should have demands to make in respect to a better adaptation of ancient formularies to present wants, such as thoughtful people count both reasonable and cogent. That a Prayer Book revised primarily for the use of a half-proscribed Church planted here and there along a sparsely inhabited sea-coast, should serve as amply as it does the purposes of a population now swollen from four millions to fifty, and covering the whole breadth of the continent, is marvel enough; to assert for the book entire adequacy to meet these altered circumstances is a mistake. "New time, new favors, and new joys," so a familiar hymn affirms, "do a new song require." We have conceded the principle so far as psalmody is concerned, why not apply it to the service of prayer as well as to that of praise, and in addition to our new hymns secure also such new intercessions and new thanksgivings as the needs of to-day suggest?

The reference in the resolution to the approaching

completion of the century has since been playfully characterized as a bit of "sentimentalism."* The criticism would be entirely just if the mere recurrence of the centennial anniversary were the point chiefly emphasized. But when a century closes as this one of ours has done with a great social revolution whereby "all estates of men" have been more or less affected, the proposal to signalize entrance upon a fresh stretch of national life by making devotional preparation for it is something better than a pretty conceit; there is a serious reasonableness in it.†

Every revision of the Common Prayer of the Church of England, and there have been four of them since Edward's First Book was put in print, has taken place at some important era of transition in the national life: and conversely it may be said that every civil crisis, with a single exception, has left its mark upon the formularies.

To one who argues that because we in this country are evidently entering upon a new phase of the national life we ought similarly to re-enforce and readjust our

---

* *Church Eclectic* for November, 1880.

† Remembering the deluge of "centennial" rhetoric let loose upon the country five years ago, another critic may well feel justified in finding in the language of the resolution what he considers "an unnecessary *raison d'être*." But it is just possible that centennial changes rest on a basis of genuine cause and effect quite independent of the decimal system. A century covers the range of three generations, and the generation is a natural, not an arbitrary division of time. What the grandfather practises the son criticises and the grandson amends. This at least ought to commend itself to the consideration of the lovers of mystical numbers and "periodic laws."

service-book, it is no sufficient reply to urge the severance effected here between Church and State. The fact that ours is a non-established Church does not make her wholly unresponsive to the shocks of change that touch the civil fabric. In so far as a political renewal alters the social grading of society, bringing in education, for instance, where before it was not, or suddenly developing new forms of industrial activity, the Church, whether established or not, is in duty bound to take cognizance of the fresh field of duty thus suddenly thrust upon her, and to prepare herself accordingly.

In the Preface added to the English Prayer Book at the Restoration, and commonly attributed to Sanderson, " that staid and well weighed man," as Hammond called him, there occurs a sentence which, both on account of its embodying in a few words the whole philosophy of liturgical revision and because of a certain practical bearing presently to be pointed out, it is worth while, in spite of its familiarity, to quote :

" The particular forms of Divine worship, and the rites and ceremonies appointed to be used therein, being things in their own nature indifferent and alterable and so acknowledged, it is but reasonable, that upon weighty and important considerations, according to the various exigency of times and occasions, such changes and alterations should be made therein, as to those that are in place of authority should from time to time seem either necessary or expedient."

Contemporaneously with this utterance there came into the Prayer Book, as a direct consequence of the enormous enlargement of the naval and commercial marine that had taken place under the Commonwealth, the "Forms of Prayer to be used at Sea." Here was a wise and right-minded recognition of a new want that had sprung up with a new time, a want which jealousy of the Puritans who had built up the naval supremacy did not prevent the Caroline bishops from meeting. But the change that passed on England during five years of Cromwell was as nothing compared with the transformation of America under ninety-five years of the federal constitution. Take a single illustration. The year 1789, the date of the Ratification of the American Prayer Book, saw sea-island cotton first planted in the United States, and it was about that time that upland cotton also began to be cultivated for home and foreign use. As the effect of this scarcely noticed experiment there straightway sprang up an industry, North and South, which has been to our country almost what her shipping interest is to Great Britain. Bishop White and his associates were not to blame for failure to provide bread that all this unanticipated multitude of toilers should eat. And yet a failure there has been. No one who has not labored at the task of trying to commend the Church of the Prayer Book to the working class, as it is represented in our large manufacturing towns, can know how lamentable that failure is. We gather in the rich and the poor, but the great middle class that makes the staple and the strength of American society stands aloof.

Nowhere in this country, for instance, has the Church had a better opportunity to show what it could do for American people than in the city of Lowell, where cotton spinning had its first large development. It was a virgin soil: the Episcopal Church, as rarely happens, was earliest on the ground: and not only so, but it enjoyed for some years the friendly protection of the proprietors of the new settlement, almost a religious monopoly—was, in fact, an ecclesiastical preserve. Moreover, this beginning antedated the Irish occupation by many years, at least so far as skilled labor was concerned, for during a considerable period the operatives in the mills were of native New England stock, the best possible material to be made over into churchmen and churchwomen. And yet notwithstanding all this, and notwithstanding the patient and unintermitted toil through more than fifty years of perhaps the most laborious parish priest on the American clergy list, the Episcopal Church has to-day but a comparatively slender hold upon the affections and loyalty of the people of this largest of the manufacturing cities of New England.

A similar failure to "reach the masses" betrays itself in Worcester and Fall River, the two cities of like character that come next in order of population, for in the former of these last named places only about two per cent of the inhabitants have affiliations of any sort with the Episcopal Church.

It was considerations of this sort, backed perhaps by memories of the ringing appeal sounded three years before at Boston by the Bishop of Connecticut, that moved the Convention to interpret as something better than a bit of sentimentalism the invitation to look the times in the face, and give the new century its infant baptism.

But besides all this there pressed upon the mind of bishops and deputies a cumulative argument of a wholly different sort. The demand for revision seemed to be closing in upon the Church on converging lines. It was plain that, before long, hands of change must necessarily be laid upon certain semi-detached portions of the Prayer Book. There was the New Lectionary, for example, that would presently be knocking for hospitable reception within the covers, and the old Easter Tables, as they now stand, could not, it was observed, last very much longer. A new book, in the publisher's sense of that term, would soon have to be made. The sanctity of stereotype plates must be disturbed. Moreover, here was an admirable opportunity to settle the wrangle, now of nine years' standing, over the best way of bringing to pass shortened services for week-day use. Add to this the fact that the intrinsic weakness of the driblet method of revision* had been

---

* The real argument against the "driblet method" (by which is meant the concession of improvement only as it is actually conquered inch by inch) lies in what has been already said about the undesirability of frequent changes in widely used formularies of worship.

It may be true, as some allege, that a revision of the Prayer Book would shake the Church, but it is more likely that half a dozen patchings at triennial intervals would shatter it. After twenty years of this sort of piecemeal revision, a *variorum* edition of the Prayer Book would be a requisite of every well furnished pew.

The late Convention has been twitted with inconsistency on the score of having negatived outright the proposal for a Commission to overhaul the Constitution of the Church while consenting to send the Prayer Book to a committee for review. Discernment would be a better word than inconsistency, for although on grounds of pure theory the Constitution and the Prayer Book seem to stand in corresponding attitudes as respects methods of amendment, in

made so abundantly plain that even its former friends wisely refrained from all attempt to urge it, and our summing up of probable motives becomes approximately complete.

II. As to the measure of authority conferred on, and scope allowed to the Committee of Twenty-one, it is possible to speak with more definiteness.

A precisian might of course, were he so disposed, take up the ground that the report of the Committee when made ought to be monosyllabic, "Yes" or "No." The wording of the resolution admits of such a construction beyond a doubt; the Joint Committee was requested to consider and report whether, etc., etc. But no one who listened to the debate on the resolution could have been left in uncertainty as to the real *animus* of the measure. The thing intended to be authorized was an experimental review, with implied reference to a limited revision at some time future, in case the fruits of the review should commend themselves to the mind of the Church.

practice the difference between the two is very wide. Triennial changes in the letter of the Constitution (and these have often been made) involve no inconvenience to anybody, for the simple reason that that document must of necessity be reprinted with every fresh issue of the Journal. Old copies do not continue in use, except as books of reference, but old Prayer Books do hold their place in parish churches, and the spectacle of congregations trying to worship in unison with books some of which contained the reading of 1880, others that of 1883, and still others that of 1886 would scarcely edify. Theoretically, let it be freely granted, the "driblet method" of amendment is the proper one for both Prayer Book and Constitution, but the fact that the Convention had eyes to see that this was a case to which the maxims of pure mathematics did not apply should be set down to its credit, rather than its discredit.

A distinction must be drawn between revision and review. Revision implies review as an antecedent step, but review is by no means necessarily followed by revision. The English book was reviewed and revised in 1662; it was reviewed but not revised in 1689. Review is tentative and advisory; revision is authoritative and final. In the present instance not an atom of power to effect binding change has been conveyed. No authority has been given to anybody to touch a line or a letter of the Prayer Book save in the way of suggestion and recommendation. Responsible action has been held wholly in reserve.

Moreover, even the pathway of review was most scrupulously hedged. Applying to the resolution the legal maxim, *expressio unius est exclusio alterius,* one sees at a glance that doctrinal change is a matter left wholly on one side. The two points to which the Committee is instructed to bend all its studies are "liturgical enrichment" and "increased flexibility of use." Whatsoever is more than these is irrelevant. Accurate distinguishment between such "enrichments" as have and such as have not a doctrinal bearing is, no doubt, a delicate point, and must be set down among the difficulties to be encountered. As such it will be considered further on. For the present the fact to be noted is that the authorized reviewers are both in honor and in duty bound to keep themselves absolutely clear of controversial bias. The movement is not a movement to alter in any slightest respect the dogmatic teaching of the Church, not a movement to unsettle foundations, not a movement toward disowning or repudiating our past, but simply and only an endeavor to make the Common

Prayer, if possible (and we are far from being sure, as yet, that it is possible), a better thing of its kind, more comprehensive, more elastic, more readily responsive to the demands of all occasions and the needs of " all sorts and conditions of men." Some who are deeply persuaded that only by doctrinal revision in one direction or another can the Prayer Book be made thoroughly to commend itself to the heart and mind of the American people will esteem the measure of change above indicated not worth the effort indispensable to the attainment of it. Be it so ; other some there are who do think the attempt well advised and who are willing to waive their own pet notions as to possible doctrinal improvements of the book for the sake of securing a *consensus* upon certain great practical improvements which come within the range of things attainable.

Certain it is that any attempt of a body of reviewers like this to disturb, even by "shadowed hint," the existing doctrinal settlement under which we are living together, would be resented by the whole Church.

There are divines among us who in the interest of a more sharply defined orthodoxy are conscientiously bent upon securing the reintroduction among our formularies of the so-called Athanasian Creed.

There are others who consider that a more damaging blow at the catholicity of our dogmatic position as a Church could scarcely be dealt.

Again, there are theologians who account the Prayer Book to be so thoroughly saturated in all its parts with the sacramental idea, that they would account it not only a piece of far-seeing statesmanship, but also a perfectly safe procedure to allow those who chose to do so to thank God after a child's baptism for the simple fact that he had thereby been " grafted into the body of Christ's Church."

• But over against these stand a much larger number who think nothing of the sort, and who would put up with the liturgical shortcomings of the Prayer Book, go without " enrichments " for a thousand years, rather than see the single word " regenerate " dropped out of the post-baptismal office.

Sensible men not a few are to be found who hold that the incoming tide of host-worship with which, as they conceive, our reformed Church is threatened can never be stayed unless some carefully contrived definition inserted in the Prayer Book shall make impossible this subtile and refined species of idolatry. But men no whit less sensible laugh them in the face, pointing to the " black rubric " and its history as evidence that between the admitted doctrine of the real presence and the disallowed tenet of transubstantiation no impervious barrier of words can possibly be run.

These illustrations of probable divergence in opinion, in case the field of doctrine were once entered, might be multiplied. The retranslation of the Nicene Creed and the more accurate punctuation of its sentences; the rendering of the word Sabbath in the Fourth Commandment into its English equivalent of Rest; the abolition of the curious misnomer under which we go on calling XXXVIII Articles XXXIX; the removal from the Catechism, or else the conversion into mother English of that sad *crux infantum*, the answer to the question, " What desirest thou of God in this prayer ? " are a few examples of less importance than those previously cited; and yet, in the case of the least of them, it is most unlikely that the advocates of change would have the show of hands in their favor, so sensitive is the mind of the Church to anything that looks in the least degree like tampering with the standards of weight and measure, the shekels of the sanctuary.

On the other hand, there are certain manifest and palpable instances of inaccuracy and, more rarely, infelicity of diction which the reviewers might very properly take occasion to amend even though such alterations could not be classified by a strict constructionist under either of the two heads " enrichment " and " flexibility." In the masterly Report of the Rev. Dr. T. W. Coit to the Joint Committee appointed by the Convention of 1841 to prepare a Standard Prayer Book,* a document of classical rank, there is more than one intimation of the hope that future reviewers would be given a larger liberty in this direction than he had himself enjoyed. He chafed, and naturally enough, under the necessity of reprinting in a "standard" book, evident and acknowledged solecisms and blunders. " We wanted," he says, "to correct one ungrammatical clause in the Consecration Prayer of the Communion Service. It is in the last sentence but one, at its close. It should be, not that he may dwell in them and they in him ; but, that he may dwell in us and we in him. The prayer is made up out of two or three others ; and anyone who will examine the parts put together will easily see how the thing was overlooked. A much greater error was overlooked elsewhere, showing that our American

* Reprinted together with a supplementary Letter in the Journal of the Convention of 1868.

compilers were not sufficiently aware of the necessity which requires that the Prayer Book should always be consistent with itself. I allude to something in the office for the Private Baptism of Children. Suppose a clergyman to avail himself of the license given in the Rubric after the certification. He will then be made to talk thus : 'As the Holy Gospel doth witness to our comfort, on this wise—Dost thou in the name of this child,'" etc.*

Other cases of evident inaccuracy, besides those referred to by this eminent critic, might be cited, even from the latest Standard Prayer Book, that of 1871. It is hard, for instance, to imagine even the veriest martinet in such matters objecting to the redress of a great wrong done on page 36 of the volume mentioned, where the prayer "to be used at the meetings of Convention" is entered under the general heading, "For malefactors after condemnation." Our ecclesiastical legislators have doubtless, like the rest of us, "erred and strayed" more than once, but to deal out to them such harsh measure as this is cruel.

A strange uncertainty would seem from the Rubric to exist with reference to the limits of the Litany. On page 554 of the Standard Prayer Book, the words, "Here endeth the Litany," occur immediately after the prayer, " We humbly beseech thee, O Father," while on page 31 the same statement is placed immediately after the minor benediction.

These are not faults for which it could ever be worth while to revise a Prayer Book, but they are blemishes

* Dr. Coit's Letter of 1868, also reprinted in Journal of that year.

of which the revisers of a Prayer Book ought to take note.

It is a graver matter to speak of infelicities of diction in a book so justly famous as the Prayer Book for its pure and wholesome English. Wordsworth's curse on

> One who would peep and botanize
> Upon his mother's grave

seems, in the judgment of many, fairly earned by the critic, whoever he may be, who ventures to suggest that in any slightest instance the language of the formularies might have been more happily phrased. But there are spots on the sun. In the prayer already referred to, that for use "at the meetings of Convention," the petition, "We beseech thee to be *present* with the council of thy Church here assembled in thy name and *presence*," does seem open to the charge of tautology if nothing worse.

It would be well if wherever the word occurs in the Prayer Book in connection with Deity the anthropomorphic plural "ears" could be replaced by the symbolic singular "ear."

Considering also the great evil of having in a formulary of worship too many things that have to be laboriously explained, it might be well if in the Litany the adjective "sudden," which ever since Hooker's day has given perpetual occasion for cavil, were to yield to "untimely," or some like word more suggestive than "sudden" of the thought clumsily expressed in the "Chapel Liturgy" by the awkward phrase, "death unprepared for." *

---

* See *Book of Common Prayer according to the use of King's Chapel, Boston.* Among the rhetorical crudities of this emasculated

It must be again remarked that these are not points for the sake of which word-fanciers would be justified in disturbing an existing order of things; they are simply instances of lesser improvements that might very properly accompany larger ones, should larger ones ever be seriously undertaken.

With so many pegs upon which controversies might be hung staring us in the face, can we think of it as at all likely that any considerable number of Churchmen assembled in committee (to say nothing of Convention) will be able to agree upon a common line of action with reference to an amendment of the formularies?

That is the very point at issue, and how it is to be decided only the event can show. Certainly in the roll of the victories of charity, a favorable result, were it achieved, would stand exceeding high.

This reflection naturally leads up to the inquiry whether there is any special reason to consider the present a happy moment to attempt within the limits already defined a revision of the Prayer Book.

Prayer Book (from the title-page of which, by the way, the definite article has been with praiseworthy truthfulness omitted) few things are worse than the following from the form for the Burial of Children, a piece of writing which in point of style would seem to savor more of the Lodge than of the Church: "My brethren, what is our life? It is as the early dew of morning that glittereth for a short time, and then is exhaled to heaven. Where is the beauty of childhood? Where is [*sic*] the light of those eyes and the bloom of that countenance?" . . . "Who is young and who is old? Whither are we going and what shall we become?" And yet the author of this mawkish verbiage probably fancied that he was improving upon the stately English of the Common Prayer. It is a warning to all would-be enrichers.

III. The argument for timeliness has been, in part, already stated. A revision will be timely, if the times imperatively demand it; and the main reasons for thinking that they do are before the reader. Something, however, is still left to be said in evidence that the movement now begun is opportune—not rudely thrust upon the Church. "To everything," saith the preacher, "there is a season, and a time to every purpose under heaven," and among the categories that follow this statement we find reckoned what answers to liturgical enrichment, for "there is," he observes, "a time to build up."

Fifty years ago a persuasive argument against attempting to amend the Prayer Book, either in text or rubrics, might have been based upon the lack of hands competent to undertake so delicate a task. Raw material, well adapted to edification, was lying about in blocks, but skilled workmen were scarce. This can hardly be said to-day. Simultaneously with the beginning of the Oxford movement, there naturally sprang up a fresh interest in liturgical studies, an interest which has gone on deepening and widening until in volume and momentum the stream has now probably reached its outer limit. The convincing citation, "There were giants in those days," with which a late bishop of one of the New England dioceses used to enforce his major premise that-wisdom died with Cranmer and his colleagues, no longer satisfies. Probably no period of corresponding length in the whole range of English Church history has shown itself so rich in the fruits of liturgical study as the fifty years that have elapsed since the introduction into the English Parliament of the first

Reform Bill.* This particular historical landmark is mentioned on account of the close connection of cause and effect between it and the remarkable movement set on foot by Newman, Pusey, Keble, and Froude. To be sure, one of the earliest utterances in the Tracts ran in these words : " Attempts are making to get the Liturgy altered. My dear brethren, I beseech you consider with

---

* A list of the more noticeable Anglican works on Liturgics published during the period named, arranged in the order of their appearance, will serve to illustrate the accuracy of the statement made above, and may also be of value to the general reader for purposes of reference

1832. Origines Liturgicæ, William Palmer. 1833–41 Tracts for the Times. 1840. Conferences on the Book of Common Prayer, Edward Cardwell. 1843. The Choral Service of the Churches of England and Ireland, John Jebb. 1844. The Ancient Liturgy of the Church of England, William Maskell. 1845. Pickering's Reprints of the Prayer Books of 1549, 1552, 1559, 1603, and 1662. 1846. Monumenta Ritualia, William Maskell. 1847. Reliquiæ Liturgicæ, Peter Hall. 1848. Fragmenta Liturgica, Peter Hall 1849. Book of Common Prayer with Notes legal and historical, A. J. Stephens Manuscript Book of Common Prayer for Ireland, A. J. Stephens. Tetralogia Liturgica, John Mason Neale 1853. Two Liturgies of Edward VI, Edward Cardwell. 1855. Principles of Divine Service, Philip Freeman. History of the Book of Common Prayer, F. Proctor. 1858 History of the Book of Common Prayer, T. Lathbury. 1859. Directorium Anglicanum, J. Purchas 1861. Ancient Collects, William Bright. 1865. Liber Precum Publicarum, Bright and Medd. 1865 The Priest's Prayer Book. 1865. History of the Book of Common Prayer, R. P. Blakeney. 1866. The Prayer Book Interleaved, Campion and Beaumont. 1866 The Annotated Book of Common Prayer, J. H. Blunt. 1870 The Liturgy of the Church of Sarum, Translated, Charles Walker 1870 The First Prayer Book of Edward VI. with the Ordinal, Walton and Medd 1872 Psalms

me whether you ought not resist the alteration of even one jot or tittle of it." *

And yet, notwithstanding this disclaimer, one of the main impulses that lay behind the whole movement represented by the Tracts was an earnest desire to quicken the life of the Church of England in the region of worship. In the *Table of the Tracts, showing their arrangement according to Subjects*, the "Liturgical" section comes first.

The present writer acknowledges but a very limited sympathy with the doctrinal motives and aims of either the earlier or the later Tractarians. But let us, above all things, be fair. With whatever prepossessions one looks back upon it, the ground traversed by the Church of England during the past fifty years cannot be otherwise regarded than as a field sown with mingled tares and wheat. Individuals will differ in judgment as to the proportion in which these two products of a common soil have coexisted, but even those who have most stoutly opposed themselves to the Oxford movement, as a whole, are fain to credit it with, at least, this one good result, the rescue of the usages of worship from slovenliness and torpor, and the establishment of a

and Litanies, Rowland Williams. 1872 Notitia Eucharistica, W. E. Scudamore. 1875-80. Dictionary of Christian Antiquities, Smith and Cheetham. 1876. First Prayer Book of Edward VI., compared with the successive Revisions, James Parker. 1877 Introduction to the History of the successive Revisions of the Book of Common Prayer, James Parker. 1878 Liturgies Eastern and Western, C. E. Hammond. 1880. The Convocation Prayer Book.

* Tract No. 3. *Thoughts respectfully addressed to the Clergy on alterations in the Liturgy*

better standard of what is seemly, reverent, and beautiful in the public service of Almighty God. Not that there have not been, even in this respect, grave errors in the direction of excess; the statement ventured is simply this, that, up to a certain point, all Churchmen agree in admitting a genuine and wholesome improvement in the popular estimate of what public worship, as such, ought to be. An immense amount of devout study has been given, during the period mentioned, by many able men to liturgical subjects, and it would be strange indeed if fifty years of searching criticism had not resulted in the detection of some few points in which formularies originally compiled to meet the needs of the sixteenth century might be better adapted to the requirements of the twentieth. Or, to put the same point in another way, has not all this searching into the mines of buried treasure, all this getting together of quarried stone (with possibly a certain surplusage of stubble) been so much labor lost, if there is never to come the recognition of a ripe moment for the Church to avail itself of the results achieved? Are the studious toils of a Palmer, a Maskell, a Neale, a Scudamore, and a Bright to go for nothing except in so far as they have been contributory to our fund of ecclesiological lore? If so, the contempt often expressed for ritual and liturgical studies by students busy with other lines of research would seem to be not wholly undeserved.

A good opportunity is now before the Church to give answer as to whether this form of investigation is or is not anything better than a species of sacred antiquarianism. Liturgiology as an aspirant for recognition among the useful sciences may be said at the present moment to be waiting for the verdict. To be sure, it can be asserted for liturgiology that to those who love it it is a study that proves itself, like poetry, "its own exceeding great reward." It is not worth while to dispute this point. Liturgiology pursued for its own sake may not be the loftiest of studies, but this, at least, can be said for it, that it is a not less respectable object of pursuit than many another specialty the devotees of which look down upon the liturgiologist with self-complacent scorn as a mere chiffonier. The forms which Christian worship has taken on in successive generations and among peoples of various blood are certainly as well worthy of analysis and classification as are the flora and fauna of Patagonia or New Zealand. But while the Patagonian naturalist secures recognition and is decorated, every jaunty man of letters feels at liberty to scoff at the liturgiologist as a laborious trifler.

Moreover, remembering that in favorite studies, as in crops, there rules a principle of rotation, fashion affecting even staid divines with its subtle influence, we may look to see presently a decline of interest in this particular department of inquiry. Especially may serious men be expected to turn their attention in other directions, should it be found that a *Non possumus* awaits every effort to make the fruits of their labor available for the nourishment of the Church's daily life. So then, instead of deferring action until liturgical knowledge shall have become more widely spread, and available liturgical material more abundant, we shall, if we are wise, perceive that only by moving promptly will it be possible in this case to take the tide at the full. Never again will opportunity be more ripe.

Another evidence of timeliness is supplied by the present pacific condition of the Church. Previous movements toward liturgical revision have been of a more or less partisan and acrimonious temper. Now for the first time we seem to be taking up this subject without the expression of a fear from any quarter that if changes are made this or that party will get the advantage of some other. The peculiar conditions that ensure this unwonted truce of God are not likely to last forever, nor is it perhaps wholly desirable that they should do so; what is desirable, and very desirable, is that we should avail ourselves of the lull to accomplish certain changes for the better, which in ordinary times the prevalent heat of friction makes impossible. The Joint Committee of Twenty-one is confidently believed to contain within itself every shade of color known to belong to the Anglican spectrum; if white light should be found to emerge, three years hence, as a result of the Committee's labors, it will be said, and truly, that never before in our history could such a blending of the rays possibly have taken place.

Still another consideration properly included under the general head of timeliness is said to have been urged with much force in the House of Bishops when the "enrichment" resolution was under discussion.

Up to the present time the Episcopal Church of this country has stood easily at the head in the matter of providing for the people a dignified and beautiful order of divine service. In fact, there has been, until lately, no one to compete. But all this is changing. Ours are no longer the only congregations in which common prayer is to be found. It is true that thus far the attempts at imitation have been rather grotesque than formidable, but such, until recently, have also been, in the judgment of foreign critics, all of our American endeavors after art. We are to consider what apt learners our quick-witted countrymen have shown themselves to be, in so much that even Christmas Day, once the *bête noire* of Puritan legislators, has come to be accounted almost a national festival, and we shall be convinced that our primacy in the field of liturgics is not an absolutely assured position. This argument is open to the criticism that it seems to lower and cheapen the whole subject by representing Anglican religion in a mendicant attitude bidding for the favor of the great American public, and vexed that others, fellow-suppliants, have stolen a good formula of appeal. Nevertheless there is a certain amount of reasonableness in this way of putting the thing. Certainly with those who reckon the liturgical mode of worship among the notes of the Church, the argument is one that ought to have marked influence; while with those who, not so persuaded, nevertheless view with pleased interest the general spread of a liturgical taste among the people of this country, seeing in it a token of better things to come, a harbinger of larger agreements than we have yet attained to, and of an approaching " consolation of Israel " once not thought possible—even with such the argument ought not to be wholly powerless.*

* One of the most curious illustrations of the spread of Anglican ideas about worship now in progress is to be found in the upspringing in the very bosom of Scottish Presbyterianism of a CHURCH SERVICE SOCIETY. Two of the publications of this Society have lately fallen in the present writer's way. They bear the imprint of

The fact that the Convocations of Canterbury and York have taken in hand and carried through a revision of the rubrics of the Prayer Book will seem to those who hold that our Church ought to advance *pari passu* with the Church of England, and no faster, another evidence of the timeliness of the American movement. Under the title of *The Convocation Prayer Book* there has lately appeared in England an edition of the Prayer Book so printed as to show how the book would read were the recommendations of York and Canterbury to go into effect. It is true that the consent of Parliament must be secured before the altered rubrics can have the force of law; but whatever may come of the rubrics recommended, the existence of the book containing them is evidence enough of a wide-spread conviction among the English clergy that change is needed.

Indeed never has this point been more powerfully put in the fewest possible words than by the brilliant, and no less logical than brilliant Bishop of Peterborough in a recent speech in the Upper House of Convocation.*
"If the Church of England wants absolute peace, she should have definite rubrics."

It is true he goes on to say that in his judgment the

Wm. Blackwood & Sons, Edinburgh, and are entitled respectively, *A Book of Common Order*, and *Home Prayer*. With questionable good taste the compilers have given to the former work a Greek and to the latter a Latin sub-title (Ευχολογιον and *Suspiria Domestica*). Both books have many admirable points, although, in view of the facts of history, there is a ludicrous side to this attempt to commend English viands to Northern palates under a thin garniture of Scottish herbs which probably has not wholly escaped the notice of the compilers themselves.

* See *The Guardian* (London), February 9, 1881.

dangers of carrying the question of rubrical revision into Parliament are greater than the evil of letting it alone, but it is to be remembered that we in this country are hampered with no Parliamentary entanglements and are free to do of our own motion, and in a quiet, orderly way, that which the Church of England can only do at the risk of something very like revolution.

But this matter of the rubrics and their susceptibility of improvement will come up later on. It seemed proper to refer to it, if no more, under the head of timeliness. If nothing else in the way of change be opportune at the present moment, it is an easy task to show that the rubrics, as they stand, cry aloud for a revision.

IV. The obstacles to be encountered by any Committee undertaking so to carry forward a review of the Prayer Book that revision may eventually result, are of two sorts; there are the inherent difficulties of the work itself, such, for instance, as that of matching the literary style of the sixteenth century writers, and there is the wholesome dread of a change for the worse which is sure to assert itself in many quarters the moment definite propositions shall have reached a point at which the "yeas and nays" are likely to be called.

Beginning, then, with the inherent difficulties, and taking them in the inverse order of arduousness, we see at once how hard it must be to secure unity and self-consistency in the revision of a book so complicated as the Common Prayer. It is like remodelling an old house. We think it a very easy matter, something that can be done in one's head, but the mistake is discovered when the new door designed to give symmetry to this room is found to have spoiled the looks of that, when the enlargement of the library turns out to have overtaxed the heating energy of the fireplace, and the ingenious staircase, instead of ending where it was expected to end, brings up against an intractable brick wall. Just such perils as these will beset anybody who ventures to disturb the adjustments of the "Prayer Book as it is" and to introduce desirable additions. But domestic architecture is not given up on account of the patient carefulness the practice of it demands, neither need Liturgical Revision be despaired of because it requires of the men who undertake it a like wisdom in looking before and after.

The really formidable barrier to revision, so far as what have been called the "inherent difficulties" are concerned, is reached when we touch style. How to handle without harming the sentences in which English religion phrased itself when English language was fresher and more fluent than it can ever be again is a serious question. The hands that seek to "enrich" may well be cautioned to take heed lest they despoil. It is to be remembered, however, in the way of reassurance that the alterations most likely to find favor with the reviewers are such as will enrich by restoring lost excellencies, rather than by introducing forms fashioned on a modern anvil.

The most sensitive critic could not, on the score of taste, find fault with the replacement in the Evening Prayer of the *Magnificat* and the *Nunc dimittis*, nor of bringing back a few of the Versicles that in the English book follow the Lord's Prayer, nor yet of our being allowed to say, "Lighten our darkness, we beseech thee, O Lord," rather than "O Lord, our Heavenly Father, by whose Almighty power we have been preserved this day." Objections to these alterations may be readily imagined, but it would be necessary to base them on other grounds than those of literary fastidiousness. In the case of enrichments like these no one could raise the cry that the faultless English of the Prayer Book had been marred.

But what shall be said of the composition of entirely new services and offices, if it should be judged expedient to give admission to any such? How can we be sure that such modern additions to the edifice would be sufficiently in keeping with the general tone of the elder architecture? It might be held to be an adequate answer to these questions to reply that if the living Church cannot now trust herself to speak out through her formularies in her natural voice as she did venture to do in the seventeenth century and the eighteenth, it must be that she has fallen into that stage of decrepitude where the natural voice is uncertain.

But, really, what ought to be said is this—that if the same canons of style that ruled the sixteenth century writers are studied and obeyed, there is no reason in the world why a result equally satisfactory with the one then attained should not be reached now. There is nothing supernatural about the English of the Prayer Book. Cranmer and his associates were not inspired. The prose style of the nineteenth century may not be as good as that of the sixteenth, but, at its best, it is vastly superior to eighteenth century style, and of this last there are already no inconsiderable specimens in the American Book of Common Prayer. The Office for the Visitation of Prisoners, for example, is so redolent of the times of the Georges, when it was composed, that it might be appropriately enough interleaved with prints out of Hogarth. A bit of Palladian architecture in a Gothic church is not more easily recognized. Many worse things might happen to the Prayer Book than that the nineteenth century should leave its impress upon the pages.

In fact, it is just as possible, if men will only think so, to use our language with effect for any good purpose to-day as it was three hundred years ago. All that is necessary is a willingness to submit to the same restrictions, and those mostly moral, that controlled the old writers; and our work, though not identical with theirs, will have the proper similarity. True, a modern author may not be able to reproduce, without a palpable betrayal of affectation and mannerism, the precise characteristics of a bygone style. Chattertons are not numerous. It is easier to secure for the brass andirons and mahogany dining chairs of our own manufacture the look of those that belonged to our grandfathers than it is to catch the tones of voices long dead; and just as good judgment dictates the wisdom of repeating the honest and thorough workmanship of the old cabinet-makers in place of slavishly imitating their patterns, so it will be well if the compilers of devotional forms for modern use seek to say what they have to say with sixteenth century simplicity rather than in sixteenth century speech. In letters, as in conduct, the supreme charm of style is the absence of self-consciousness. "Say in plain words the thing you mean, and say it as if you meant it," is good advice to any seeker after rhetorical excellence, be he young or old. The Reformers, that is to say, the men who Englished the Prayer Book, in seeking to meet the devotional needs of the people of their own time do not seem to have been at pains to tie themselves to the diction of a previous generation. They dared to "call a spade a spade" whenever and wherever the tool came into use, and they have their reward in the permanence of their work. Sweetnesses and prettinesses they banished altogether. Indeed, in those days it seems not to have occurred to people that such things had anything to do with religion. It was not that they did not know how to talk in the sweet way—never has sentimentalism been more rife in general literature than then, but they would not talk in that way; the stern traditions of Holy Church throughout all the world forbade. Religion was a most serious thing to their minds, and they would speak of it most seriously or not at all.

Never since language began to be used have severity and tenderness been more marvellously blended than in the older portions of the English Prayer Book.

This effect is largely due to an almost entire abstention on the part of the writers from figurative language, or at least from all imagery that is not readily recognized as Scriptural. Bread and beef are what men demand for a steady diet. Sweetmeats are well enough, now and then, but only now and then.

It is the failure to observe this plain canon of style that has made shipwreck of many an attempt to construct liturgies *de novo*. Ambitious framers of forms of worship seem almost invariably to forget that there may be such a thing as a too exquisite prayer, an altogether too "eloquent address to the throne of grace." The longest and fullest supplicatory portion of the Prayer

Book, the Litany, does not contain, from the first sentence to the last,* one single figurative expression, it is literally plain English from beginning to end; but could language be framed more intense, more satisfying, more likely to endure?

Scriptural metaphor, whether because it comes to us with the stamp of authority or on account of some subtle intrinsic excellence, it may be difficult to say, does not pall upon the taste. And yet even this is used sparingly in the Prayer Book, some of the most striking exceptions to the general rule being afforded by the collects for the first and third Sundays in Advent, the collects for the Epiphany and Easter Even, and the opening prayer in the Baptismal Office. All these are instances of strictly Scriptural metaphor, and moreover it is to be kept in mind that they are designed for occasional, not constant use. In the orders for daily Morning and Evening Prayer, the "lost sheep" of the General Confession and the "dew" of God's blessing in the Collect for Clergy and People are almost the sole, if not the sole cases of evident metaphor, and these again are Scriptural. When in Jeremy Taylor's prayer, introduced by the American revisers into the Order for the Visitation of the Sick, we come upon the comparison of human life to a "vale of misery" we feel that somehow we have struck a new current in the atmosphere; for the moment it is the rhetorician who speaks, and no longer the earnest seeker after God.

Besides this freedom from figures of speech, we notice in the style of Prayer Book English a careful

* Unless "finally to beat down Satan under our feet," be reckonéd an exception.

avoidance of whatever looks like a metaphysical abstraction. The aim is ever to present God and divine things as realities rather than as mere concepts or notions of the mind. So far as the writer remembers, not a single prayer in the whole book begins with that formula so dear to the makers of extemporary forms of devotion, "O Thou." On the contrary, the approach to the Divine Majesty is almost always made with a reference to some attribute or characteristic that links Deity to man and man's affairs; it is "O God, the Protector of all that trust in thee," or "Almighty and everlasting God who of thy tender love toward mankind," or "Lord of all power and might who art the author and giver of all good things."

Cardinal Newman in one of his theological works written before his departure from the Church of England, has a powerful passage bearing upon this point. He is criticising the evangelicals for their one-sided way of setting forth what it must mean to "preach the Gospel." No less a person than Legh Richmond is the object of his strictures.

"A remarkable contrast between our Church's and this false view of religion," he says, "is afforded in the respective modes of treating a death-bed in the Visitation of the Sick, and a popular modern work, the Dairyman's Daughter. The latter runs thus: My dear friend, do you not FEEL *that you are supported?* The Lord deals very gently with me, she replied. Are not his promises *very precious to you?* They are all yea and amen in Christ Jesus. . Do you experience any *doubts or temptations* on the subject of your eternal safety? No, sir; the Lord deals very gently with me and gives me peace. What are your *views* of the dark valley of death now that you are passing through it? *It is not dark.* Now, if it be said that such questions and answers are not only in their place innocent but natural and beautiful, I answer that this is not the point, but this, viz., they are evidently intended, whatever their merits, as a pattern of *what death-bed examinations should be.* Such is the Visitation of the Sick in the nineteenth century. Now let us listen to the nervous and stern tone of the sixteenth. In the Prayer Book the minister is instructed to say to the person visited : Forasmuch as after this life there is an account to be given to the *Righteous Judge* . . . I require you to examine yourself and your estate both toward God and man. Therefore I shall rehearse to you the *Articles of our Faith,* that you may know whether you do believe as a Christian man should or no. . . 'Then shall the minister examine whether he repent him truly of his sins, and be in *charity* with all the world : exhorting him to forgive from the bottom of his heart all persons who have offended him, and if he hath offended any other to *ask their forgiveness,* and where he hath done injury or wrong to any man that he *make amends* to the utmost of his power.' . . Such is the contrast between the dreamy talk of modern Protestantism, and 'holy fear's stern glow' in the Church Catholic." *

In this striking, though perhaps somewhat unnecessarily harsh way, Newman brings out a point which is unquestionably true, namely, that the language of the Prayer Book is of the sort which it is just now the fashion to call realistic, that is, a language conversant

* *Lectures on Justification,* p 330.

with great facts rather than with phases of feeling and
moods of mind ; which after all is only another way of
saying that it is a Book of *Common* Prayer and not a
manual for the furtherance of spiritual introspection.

These, then, are the characteristics of the Prayer Book
style : it is simple, straightforward, unmetaphorical,
realistic. Seriously it looks almost like a studied insult
alike to the scholarship and to the religion of our day, to
say that these are excellencies attainable no longer.
That revisers venturing upon additions to the Prayer
Book would be bound to set the face as a flint against
any slightest approach to sentimentality is true. But
why assume that the men do not exist who are capable
of such a measure of self-control ? Grant that there are
whole volumes of devotional matter, original and compiled, which one may ransack without finding a single
form that is not either prolix, wishy-washy, or superstitious—it does not follow that if the Prayer Book is
to be enriched, the enrichments must necessarily come
from such sources. Moreover it is to be remembered
that there is another vice of style to be shunned in
liturgical composition quite as carefully as sentimentality, namely, jejuneness. We cannot escape being
sentimental simply by being dull. Feeling must not be
denied its place in prayer for fear that it may not prove
itself a duly chastened feeling. There ought to be a
heart of fire underneath the calm surface of every
formulary of worship. Flame and smoke are out of
place ; but a liturgy should glow throughout. Coldness,
pure and simple, has no place in devotion.

Over and above the intrinsic difficulties in the way of
revision growing out of the delicate nature of the work

itself, obstacles of a different sort are certain to be encountered. In so large a body of men as the Joint Committee of the two Houses, entire and cordial agreement is almost too much to be expected; and then even supposing a unanimous report submitted, what is likely to follow? Why this—if the changes proposed are few, the cry will be raised, It surely is not worth while to alter the Prayer Book for the sake of so insignificant a gain; whereas if the changes proposed are considerable, the counter cry will be sounded, This is revolution.

Then there is the anxious question, How will it look to the English? What will be the effect on the *Concordat* if we touch the Prayer Book? To be sure, the *Concordat* does not seem to weigh very heavily on the shoulders of the other party, as indeed there is no reason why it should. Convocation does not much disturb itself as to the view General Convention is likely to take of its sayings and doings, and even disestablishment might proceed without our being called into consultation. And yet the *Concordat* difficulty will have to be reckoned with; and the dire spectre of a possible disowning of us by our mother the Church of England will have to be laid, before any alterations in the Book of Common Prayer will be accounted by some among us perfectly safe.

But it is scarcely worth while to go on gratuitously suggesting opposition arguments. They will be sure to present themselves unsolicited in due time. For the present it is enough to add that if the movement for liturgical revision has not in it enough toughness of fibre to enable it to survive vigorous attack, it does not deserve success.

V. Under the head of liturgical enrichment ought to be classed whatever alteration would really serve to enhance the beauty, majesty, or fitness, of accepted formularies of worship. Excision may, under conceivable circumstances, be enrichment. James Wyatt undoubtedly imagined that he was improving the English cathedrals when he whitewashed their interiors, added composition pinnacles to the west towers of Durham, and rearranged the ancient monuments of Salisbury; but an important part of the enrichment accomplished by our nineteenth century restorers has lain simply in the undoing of what Wyatt did.

Again, substitution may be enrichment, as in the case where a wooden spire built upon a stone tower is taken down to be replaced by honest work. It would be an enrichment if in St. George's Chapel, the central shrine of British royalty, the sham insignia now overhanging the stalls of the knights of the garter were to give room to genuine armor. Not merely then by addition, but possibly, in some instances, by both subtraction and substitution, we may find "the Prayer-book as it is" open to improvement.

Before, however, entering upon any criticism of the formularies in detail, it is important to draw a distinction between two very different things, namely, the structure of a liturgical office and the contents of it. By structure should be understood the skeleton or frame that makes the groundwork of any given office, by contents the actual liturgical material employed in filling out the office to its proper contour.

The offices of the Roman Breviary, for example, continue, for the most part, identical in structure from day to day, the year through; but they vary in contents. For an illustration nearer home take our own *Order for Daily Morning Prayer*. The structure of it is as follows: 1. Sentences, 2. Exhortation, 3. Confession, 4. Absolution, 5. Lord's Prayer, 6. Versicles, 7. Invitatory Psalm, 8. The Psalms for the day, 9. Lection, 10. Anthem or Canticle, 11. Lection, 12. Anthem or Canticle, 13. Creed, 14. Versicles, 15. Collect for the day, 16. Stated Collects and Prayers, 17. Benediction

Now it is evident that without departing by a hair's breadth from the lines of this framework, an indefinite number of services might by a process of substitution be put together, each one of which would in outward appearance differ widely from every other one. The identical skeleton, that is to say, might be so variously clothed upon that no two of its embodiments would be alike. But is it desirable to run very much after variety of such a sort in a book of prayer designed for common use? Most assuredly, No. To jeopard the supreme *desideratum* in a people's manual of worship, simplicity: to make it any harder than it now is for the average "stranger in the Church" to find the places, would be on the part of revisionists an unpardonable blunder.

There are, however, a few points at which the Morning Prayer might advantageously be enriched, and no risk run. It would surely add nothing to the difficulty of finding the places if for one-half of the present opening sentences there were to be substituted sentences appropriate to special days and seasons of the ecclesiastical year. We should in this way be enabled to give the key-note of the morning's worship at the very outset. Having once departed, as in the case of our first two sentences, from the English precedent of putting only penitential verses of Scripture to this use, there is no reason why we should not carry out still more fully in our selection the principle of appropriateness. The sentences displaced need not be lost, for they might still stand, as now, at the opening of the Evening Prayer.

Passing on to the declarations of absolution there is an opportunity to simplify the arrangement by omitting the alternate form borrowed from the Order for the Administration of the Lord's Supper, where only it properly belongs. This, however, is a change likely to be resisted on doctrinal grounds, and need not be urged.

Coming to the *Venite*, we find another opportunity to accentuate the Christian Year. It may be said that the rubric, as it is already written, allows for the substitution of special anthems on the greater festivals and fasts. This is true; but by giving the anthem for Easter a place of honor, while relegating anthems for the other great days to an unnoticed spot between the Selections and the Psalter, the American compilers did practically discriminate in favor of Easter and against the rest. The real needs of the case would be more wisely met if the permission to omit *Venite* now attached to "the nineteenth day of the month" were to be extended to Ash-Wednesday and Good Friday, and special New Testament anthems analagous to the Easter one were to be inserted along with the respective Collects, Epistles, and Gospels, for Christmas-day and Whitsunday.

By this change we should put each of the three great festivals of the year into possession of an invitatory anthem of its own; and we should obviate on the fasting days, by the simple expedient of omission, the futile efforts of choir-master and organist to transform *Venite* from a cry of joy into a moan of grief.

This brings us to the Psalter. Here we have an opportunity to correct the palpable blunder by which it has come about that the greatest of the penitential psalms, the fifty-first, has no place assigned it among the proper psalms either for Ash-Wednesday or for Good Friday.* It would also be well to make optional, if not obligatory, the use of "proper psalms" on days other than those already provided with them; *e. g.*, Advent Sunday, the Epiphany, Easter Even, Trinity Sunday, and All Saints' Day.† There would be a still larger gain in the direction of "flexibility of use," as well as a great economy of valuable space, if instead of reprinting some thirty of the Psalms of David under the name of Selections, we were to provide for allowing "select" psalms to be announced by number in the same manner that "proper" psalms are now announced. Instead of only the ten selections we now have, there might then be made available twenty or thirty groups of psalms at absolutely no sacrifice of room. It has been objected to this proposal that the same difficulty which now attaches to the finding of the "proper psalms" on great days would embarrass congregations whenever "select

---

*The rationale of this curious lapse is simple The American revisers, instead of transferring the Commination Office *in toto* to the new book, wisely decided to engraft certain features of it upon the Morning Prayer for Ash-Wednesday. In the process, the fifty-first Psalm, which has a recognized place in the Commination, dropped out, instead of being transferred, as it should have been, to the proper psalms.

† See the Convocation Prayer Book.

psalms" were given out; but this is fairly met by the counter consideration that if our people were to be educated by the use of select psalms into a more facile handling of the Psalter it would be just so much gained for days when the "proper psalms" must of necessity be found and read. The services, that is to say, would run all the more smoothly on the great days, after congregations had become habituated, on ordinary days, to picking out the psalms by number.

Another step in the line of simplification, and one which it is in order to mention here, would be the removal from the Morning Prayer of *Gloria in Excelsis*, seeing that it is never, or almost never, sung at the end of the psalms unless at Evening Prayer. As to the expediency of restoring what has been lost of *Benedictus* after the second lesson, the present writer offers no opinion. There are some who warmly advocate the replacement, and there is, unquestionably, much to be said in favor of it. It is unlikely that any doctrinal motive dictated the abbreviation.

Pausing a moment at the Creeds for the insertion of a better title than "*Or this*" before the confession of Nicæa, we pass to the versicles that follow.

Here again it would be enrichment to restore the words of the English book, although the task of finding an equally melodious equivalent for *O Lord, save the Queen* might not be easy.

Happily the other versicles are such as no civil revolution can make obsolete. It will never be amiss to pray,

Endue thy ministers with righteousness.
Answer. *And make thy chosen people joyful.*

These are all the alterations for which the present Morning Prayer considered as a form of Divine Service for Sundays would seem to call. It will be observed that they are far from being of a radical character, that they affect the structure of the office not at all, and touch the contents of it but slightly.

The case is altered when we come to the Order for Evening Prayer. Here there is a demand, not indeed for any structural change, but for very decided enrichment by substitution. The wording of the office is altogether too exact an echo of what has been said only a few hours before in Morning Prayer. It betokens a poverty of resources that does not really exist, when we allow ourselves thus to exhort, confess, absolve, intercede, and give thanks in the very same phrases at three in the afternoon that were on our lips at eleven in the morning.

Doubtless liturgical worship owes a good measure of its charm to the subtle power of repetition; but the principle is one that must be handled and applied with the most delicate tact, or virtue goes out of it. We must distinguish between similarity and sameness. The ordered recurrence of accents is what makes the rhythm of verse; but for all that, there is a difference between poetry and sing-song, just as there is a difference between melody and monotony. Moreover, the taste of mankind undergoes change as to the sorts of repetition which it is disposed to tolerate. No modern poet of standing would venture, for instance, to employ identical epithets to the extent that Homer does, making Aurora "rosy-fingered" every time she appears upon the scene, and Juno as invariably "ox-eyed." People were pleased with it then, they would not be pleased with it now. It is possible in liturgics so to employ the principle of repetition that no wearying sense of sameness will be conveyed, and again it is possible so to mismanage it as to transform worship into something little better than a "slow mechanic exercise." Mere iteration, as such, is barren of spiritual power; witness the endless sayings over of *Kyrie Eleison* in the Oriental service-books, a species of vain repetition which a liturgical writer of high intelligence rightly characterizes as "unmeaning, if not profane."* Now the common popular criticism upon the Evening Prayer of the Church is that it repeats too slavishly the wording of the Morning Prayer. If this is an unjust criticism we ought not to let ourselves be troubled by it. On the other hand, if it is a just criticism it will be much wiser of us to heed than to stifle the voice that tells us the truth. It might seem to be straining a point were one to venture to explain the present very noticeable disinclination of Churchmen to attend a second service on Sunday, by connecting it with the particular infelicity in question; but that the excuse, We have said all this once to-day; why say it again? may possibly have something, even if not much, to do with the staying at home is certainly a fair conjecture.

Without altering at all the structure of the Evening Prayer, it would be perfectly possible so to refill or reclothe that formulary as to give it the one thing needful which now it lacks—freshness. In such a process the *Magnificat* and the *Nunc dimittis* would play an important part; as would also certain "ancient collects" of

* *Prayer Book Interleaved*, p. 65.

which we have heard much of late. Failing this, the next best thing (and the thing, it may be added, much more likely to be done, considering what a tough resistant is old usage) would be the provision of an alternate and optional form of Evening Prayer, to be used either in lieu of, or as supplementary to the existing office. In the framing of such a *Later Evensong* a larger freedom would be possible than in the refilling of a form the main lines of which were already fixed. Still, the first plan would be better, if only it could be brought within the range of things possible.

Next to Evening Prayer in the order of the Table of Contents comes the Litany. Here there is no call for enrichment,* though increased flexibility of use might

---

* A curious illustration of the sensitiveness of the Protestant Episcopal mind to anything that can be supposed even remotely to endanger our doctrinal settlement was afforded at the late General Convention, when the House of Deputies was thrown into something very like a panic by a most harmless suggestion with reference to the opening sentences of the Litany. A venerable and thoroughly conservative deputy from South Carolina had ventured to say that it would be doctrinally an improvement if the tenet of the double procession of the Holy Ghost were to be removed from the third of the invocations, and a devotional improvement if the language of the fourth were to be phrased in words more literally Scriptural and less markedly theological than those at present in use. Eager defenders of the faith instantly leaped to their feet in various parts of the House, persuaded that a deadly thrust had been aimed at the doctrine of the Trinity. Never was there a more gratuitous misconception. The real intrenchment of the doctrine of the Trinity, so far as the Litany is concerned, lies in the four opening words of the second and the five opening words of the third of the invocations, and these it had not been proposed to touch. In confirmation of this view of the

be secured for this venerable form of intercessory prayer by prefixing to it the following rubric abridged from a similar one proposed in The Convocation Prayer Book :

"*A General Supplication, to be sung or said on Sundays, Wednesdays, and Fridays, and on the Rogation Days, after the third collect at Morning or Evening Prayer, or before the Administration of the Holy Communion; or as a separate Service.*

"NOTE.—*The Litany may be omitted altogether on Christmas Day, Easter Day, and Whitsunday.*"

In connection with the Morning and Evening Service there is another important question that imperatively

matter, it is pertinent to instance the *Book of Family Prayers* lately put forth by a Committee of the Upper House of the Convocation of Canterbury. This manual provides no fewer than six different Litanies, all of them opening with addresses to the three Persons of the adorable Trinity, and yet in no one instance is the principle advocated by the deputy from South Carolina unrecognized. Every one of the six Litanies begins with language similar to that which he recommended. [See also in witness of the mediæval use, which partially bears out Mr McCrady's thought, the ancient Litany reprinted by Maskell from *The Prymer in English.* Mon Rit. ii. p. 95] If the Upper House of the Convocation of Canterbury, fondly supposed by us Anglicans to be the very citadel of sound doctrine, be thus tainted with heresy, upon what can we depend ?

Polemical considerations aside, probably even the most orthodox would allow that the invocations of the Litany might gain in devotional power, while losing nothing in august majesty, were the third to run—*O God the Holy Ghost, Sanctifier of the faithful, have mercy upon us miserable sinners* And the fourth as in Bishop Heber's glorious hymn, *Holy, Holy, Holy, Lord God Almighty, have mercy upon us miserable sinners.* But all this is doctrinal and plainly *ultra vires.*

demands discussion, namely, a week-day worship. The movement for "shortened services," so-called, has shared the usual fate of all efforts at bettering the life of the Church, in being at the outset of its course widely and seriously misunderstood. The impression has gone abroad, and to-day holds possession of many otherwise well-informed people, that a large and growing party in the Episcopal Church has openly declared itself wearied out with overmuch prayer and praise. Were such indeed the fact, the scandal would be grave; but the real truth about the matter is that the promoters of shortened services, instead of seeking to diminish, are really eager to see multiplied the amount of worship rendered in our churches. "Shortened services" is a phrase of English, not American origin, and has won its way here by dint of euphony rather than of fitness. Readjusted services, though a more clumsy, would be a less misdirecting term. In the matter of Sunday worship, the liberty now generally conceded of using separately the Morning Prayer, the Litany, and the Holy Communion is all that need be asked. Whether these services, or at least two of them, do not in themselves admit of a certain measure of improvement is a point that has already been considered, but there certainly is no need of shortening them, whatever else it may be thought well to do. When what a Boston worthy once termed "a holy alacrity" is observed, on the part of both minister and singers, even the aggregated services of Morning Prayer, Litany, and "Ante-Communion," together with a sermon five-and-twenty minutes long, can easily be brought within the compass of an hour and a half—a measure of time not unreasonably large to be given to the principal occasion of worship on the Lord's Day. As for the Evening Prayer—there certainly ought to be no call for the shortening of that on Sundays; for it would be scarcely decent or proper to devote to such a service anything less than the half hour the existing office demands.

What the advocates of shortened services really desire to see furthered is an increase in the frequency of opportunities for worship during the week, their conviction being that if the Church were to authorize brief services for morning and evening use, such as would not occupy much more time than family prayers ordinarily do, the attendance might be secured of many who, at present, put aside the whole question of going to church on week-days as impracticable. Supposing it could be proved that such a provision would work to the discouragement of family prayer, it would plainly be wrong to advocate it; no priesthood is more sacred than that which comes with fatherhood. But we must face the fact that in our modern American life family prayer, like sundry other wholesome habits, has fallen largely into disuse. If the Church can, in any measure, supplement the deficiencies of the household, and help to supply to individuals a blessing they would gladly enjoy at their own homes, if they might, it is her plain duty to do so. Moreover, many a minister who single-handed cannot now prudently undertake a daily service, as that is commonly understood, would acknowledge himself equal to the less extended requirement.

Not a few careful and friendly observers of the practical working of Anglican religion have been reluctantly led to consider the daily service, as an institution, only meagrely successful. Looking at the matter historically we find no reason to wonder at such a conclusion.

Our existing usage (or more correctly, perhaps, *nonuser*) dates from the Reformation period. The English Church and nation of that day had grown up familiar with the spectacle of a very large body of clerics, secular and regular, whose daily occupation may be said to have been the pursuit of religion.* The religion pursued consisted chiefly in the saying of prayers, and very thoroughly, so far at least as the consumption of time was concerned, were the prayers said. What more natural than that, under such circumstances, and with such associations, the compilers of a common Prayer Book for the people should have failed to see any good reason for discriminating between the amount of service proper to the Lord's Day and the amount that might be reasonably expected on other days? Theoretically they were right, all time belongs to God and he is as appropriately worshipped on Tuesdays and Thursdays as on Sundays. And yet as a result of their making no such discrimination, we have the daily service on our hands—a comparative, even if not an utter failure. We may lament the fact, but a fact it is, that in spite of all its improved appliances for securing leisure, the world is busier than ever it was ; and there will always be those who will insist that the command to labor on six days is as imperative as the injunction to rest upon the seventh. As a consequence of all this accelerated business, and of the diminution in the number of persons officially set apart

---

* A very natural explanation, by the way, of the fact, often noticed, that there is no petition in the Litany for an increase of the ministry.

for prayer, the unabridged service of the Church fails to command a week-day attendance. We have no "clerks" nowadays to fill the choir. The only clerks known to modern times are busy at their desks.

It may be urged in reply to this that the practical working of the daily service ought to be kept a secondary consideration, and that its main purpose is symbolical, or representative; the priest kneeling in his place, day by day, as a witness that the people, though unable personally to be present, do, in heart and mind, approve of a daily morning and evening sacrifice of prayer. This conception of the daily service as a vicarious thing has a certain mystical beauty about it, but if it is to be adopted as the Church's own let us, at least, clear ourselves of inconsistency by striking out the word "common" from before the word "prayer" in characterizing our book.

What is really needed for daily use in our parishes is a short form of worship specially framed for the purpose. If they could be employed without offence to the Protestant ear (and they are good English Reformation words) *Week-Day Matins* and *Week-Day Evensong* would not be ill chosen names for such services. The framework of these Lesser Orders for Morning and Evening Prayer, as they might also be called, were the other titles found obnoxious, ought to be modelled upon the lines of the existing daily offices, though with a careful avoidance of identity in contents. There should be, for instance, as unvarying elements, the reading of the lessons for the day, the use of the collect for the day, and the saying or singing of the psalms for the day. Another constant would be the Lord's Prayer;

but aside from these the *Lesser Order* need have nothin common with the Order as we have it now. There might be, for example, after the manner of the old service-books, an invitatory opening with versicles and responses, or if the present mode of opening by sentences were preferred, specially chosen sentences, different from those with which the Sunday worship has made us familiar, could be employed. Moreover, the anthems or canticles and the prayers, with the exception of the two just mentioned, ought also to be distinctive, and, in the technical sense of the word, *proper* to the week-day use.

Again, it would serve very powerfully and appropriately to emphasize the pivot points in the ritual year if this same principle were to be applied to saints' days, and we were to have special *Holyday Matins* and *Holyday Evensong*, there still being required, on the greater festivals and fasts, the normal Morning and Evening Prayer proper to the Lord's Day.*

The argument in favor of thus specializing the services for week-days and holydays, in preference to fol-

* Here, *i. e.*, in connection with Saints' Day services, would be an admirable opportunity for the introduction into liturgical use of the Beatitudes. What could possibly be more appropriate? And yet these much loved words of Christ have seldom been given the place in worship they deserve

They do find recognition as an antiphon in the *Liturgy of St. Chrysostom* To reassert a usage associated in the history of liturgics with the name of this Father of the Church and with his name only, would be to pay him better honor than we now show by three times inserting in our Prayer Book the collect conjecturally his—a thing the Golden-mouthed himself, when in the flesh, would not have dreamed of doing. "Once," he would have said, "is enough."

lowing the only method heretofore thought possible, namely, that of shortening the Lord's Day Order, rests on two grounds. In the first place permissions to skip and omit are of themselves objectionable in a book of devotions. They have an uncomely look. Our American Common Prayer boasts too many disfigurements of this sort already.

Such a rubric as *The minister may, at his discretion, omit all that follows to, etc*, puts one in mind of the finger-post pointing out a short cut to weary travellers. It is inopportune thus to hint at exhaustion as the probable concomitant of worship. That each form should have an integrity of its own, should as a separate whole be either said complete or left unsaid, is better liturgical philosophy than any "shortened services act" can show.

In the second place, a certain amount of variety would be secured by the proposed method which under the existing system we miss. There is, of course, such a danger as that of providing too much liturgical variety. Amateur makers of Prayer Books almost invariably fall into this slough. Hymn-books, as is well known, often destroy their own usefulness by including too many hymns; and Prayer Books may do the same by having too many prayers.*

To transgress in the compiling of formularies the line of average memory, to provide more material than the mind of an habitual worshipper is likely to assimilate, is to misread human nature. But here, as elsewhere, there is a just mean. Cranmer and his colleagues in the work of revision jumped at one bound from a scheme which

* *The Priest's Prayer Book* has 688 (!!) mostly juiceless

provided a distinctive set of services for every day in the year to a scheme that assigned one stereotyped form to all days.

Now nothing could be more unwise than any attempt to restore the methods of the Breviary, with its complicated and artificial forms of devotion; but so far to imitate the Breviary as to provide within limits for a recognition of man's innate love of change would be wisdom. By having a distinctive service for week-days, and a distinctive service for holydays, we might add just that little increment to the Church's power of traction that in many instances would avail to change "I cannot go to church this morning" into "I cannot stay away."

It will be urged as a counter-argument to these considerations that the thing is impossible, that such a measure of enrichment is entirely in excess of anything the Church has expressed a wish to have, and that for reviewers to propose a plan so sweeping would be suicide. Doubtless this might be a sufficient answer to anybody who imagined that by a bare majority vote of two successive General Conventions new formularies of daily worship could be forced upon the Church. But suppose such formularies were to be made *optional;* suppose there were to be given to parishes the choice between these three things, viz.: (*a*) the normal Morning Prayer; (*b*) a shortened form of the normal Morning Prayer; and (*c*) such a special order as has been sketched—what then? Would the Church's liberty be impaired! On the contrary, would not the borders of that liberty have been most wisely and safely widened by the steady hand of law?

This is perhaps the right point at which to call attention to the present state of the "shortened services" controversy, for wearisome as the story has become by frequent repetition, the *nexus* between it and the subject in hand is too important to be left out of sight.

In the General Convention of 1877, where the topic under its American aspects was for the first time thoroughly discussed, the two Houses came to a deadlock. The deputies on the one hand, almost to a man, voted in favor of giving the desired relief by rubric, thus postponing for three years' time the fruition of their wish; while the bishops with a unanimity understood to have been equally striking insisted that a simple canon, such as could be passed at once, would suffice. And so the subject dropped.

At the late Convention of 1880 an eirenicon was discovered. The quick eye of one of the legal members of the House of Deputies detected on the fourth page of the Prayer Book, just opposite the Preface, a loophole of escape, to wit, *The Ratification of the Book of Common Prayer*. Here was the very *tertium quid* whereby the common wish of both parties to the dispute might be effected without injury to the sensibilities of either.

The *Ratification* certainly did not look like a canon; neither could anybody with his eyes open call it a rubric—why not amend that, and say no more about it? The suggestion prevailed, and by a vote of both Houses, the following extraordinary document is hereafter to stand (the next General Convention consenting) in the very fore-front of the Prayer Book :

THE RATIFICATION OF THE BOOK OF COMMON PRAYER.

By the Bishops, the Clergy, and the Laity of the Protestant Episcopal Church in General Convention assembled.

"The General Convention of the Church having heretofore, to wit : on the sixteenth day of October in the year A. D. 1789, set forth *a Book of Common Prayer and Administration of the Sacraments and other Rites and Ceremonies of the Church,* and thereby established the said book, and declared it to be the Liturgy of said Church, and required that it be received as such by all the members of the same and be in use from and after the first day of October in the year of our Lord 1790 ; the same book is hereby ratified and confirmed, and ordered to be the use of this Church from this time forth.

" But note, however, that on days other than Sundays, Christmas-day, the Epiphany, Ash-Wednesday, Good Friday, and Ascension Day, it shall suffice if the Minister begins Morning or Evening Prayer at the General Confession or the Lord's Prayer preceded by one or more of the Sentences appointed at the beginning of Morning and Evening Prayer, and end after the Collect for Grace or the Collect for Aid against Perils, with 2 Cor. xiii. 14, using so much of the Lessons appointed for the day and so much of the Psalter as he shall judge to be for edification.

" And note also that on any day when Morning and Evening Prayer shall have been duly said or are to be said, and on days other than those first aforementioned, it shall suffice, when need may require, if a sermon or lecture be preceded by at least the Lord's Prayer and one or more Collects found in this book, provided that no prayers not set forth in said book, or otherwise authorized by this Church, shall be used before or after such sermon or lecture.*

"And note further also that on any day the Morning Prayer, the Litany, or the Order for the Administration of the Lord's Supper may be used as a separate and independent service, provided that no one of these services shall be disused habitually."

It may seem harsh to characterize this act as the mutilation of a monument; but really it does seem to be little else. The old Ratification of 1789 is an historic landmark; it is the sign-manual of the Church of

---

* In connection with this clause there sprang up an animated and interesting debate in the House of Deputies as to the wisdom of thus seeming to cut off every opportunity for extemporary prayer in our public services. Up to this time, it was alleged, a liberty had existed of using *after* sermon, if the preacher were disposed to do so, the "free prayer" which *before* sermon it was confessedly not permitted him to have—why thus cut off peremptorily an ancient privilege? why thus sharply annul a traditional if not a chartered right?

At first sight this distinction between before and after sermon looks both arbitrary and artificial, but when examined there is found to be a reason in it. The sermon, especially in the case of emotional preachers, is a sort of bridge of transition from what we may call the liturgical to the spontaneous mood of mind, and if the speaker has carried his listeners with him they are across the bridge at the same moment with himself. The thing that would have been incongruous before, becomes natural after the minister has been for some time speaking less in his priestly than in his personal character.

The notion that the points at issue between the advocates of liturgical and the advocates of extemporaneous worship can be settled by a promiscuous jumbling together of the two modes, is a fond conceit, as the Reformed Episcopalians will doubtless confess

White's and Seabury's day, and ought never to be disturbed or tampered with while the Prayer Book stands. The year 1889 might very properly see a supplemental Ratification written under it; and testifying to the fact of Revision; but to write into that venerable text

when they shall have had time enough to make full trial of the following rubrics in their Prayer-book:

¶ *Then shall the Minister say the Collects and Prayers following in whole or in part, or others at his discretion.*

¶ *Here may be used any of the occasional Prayers, or extemporaneous Prayer.*

This is bad philosophy. It need not be said that such directions are undevotional—for doubtless they were piously meant; but it must be said that they are inartistic (if the word may be allowed), at variance with the fitness of things and counter to the instinct of purity. Formality and informality are two things that cannot be mingled to advantage. There is place and time for each. The secret of the power of liturgical worship is wrapped up with the principle of order. A certain majesty lies in the movement which is without break. On the other hand the charm of extemporaneous devotion, and it is sometimes a very real charm, is traceable to our natural interest in whatever is irregular, fresh, and spontaneous.

To suppose that we can secure at any given time the good effects of both methods by some trick of combination is an error—as well attempt to arrange on the same plot of ground a French and an English garden. If indeed Christian people could bring themselves to acknowledge frankly the legitimacy of both methods and provide amicably for their separate use, a great step forward in the direction of Church unity would have been achieved; but for a catholicity so catholic as this, public opinion is not yet ripe, and perhaps may not be ripe for centuries to come. Those who believe in the excellency of liturgies, while not believing in them as *jure divino*, would be well content in such a case to wait the working of the principle of the survival of the fittest.

special directions as to what may be done on days other than Ash-Wednesday, and what must not be done without 2 Cor. xiii. 14, is very much as if the City Government of Cambridge should cause to be cut upon the stone under the Washington elm which now records the fact that there the commander of the American armies first drew his sword, divers and sundry additional items of information, such as the distance to Watertown, the shortest path across the common, etc., etc.

Why the Convention after having entrusted to a Joint Committee, by a decisive vote, the task of devising means for securing for the Prayer Book "increased flexibility of use," should have thought it necessary subsequently to take up with this compromise of a compromise (for such the proposal to amend the Ratification really is) it is difficult to say. Perhaps it was with the determination to have, at any rate, something to fall back upon in case the larger and more comprehensive measure should come to naught.

The *rubric* is confessedly the proper place for directions as to how to use the services, and but for the very natural and defensible objection on the part of some to touching the Prayer Book at all, there never would have been any question about it.* This objection having

* The able and fair minded jurist who first hit upon this ingenious scheme for patching the Ratification has lately, with characteristic frankness, said substantially this under his own signature.

"The proper place for the amendment," he writes, "is at the end of the first rubric preceding the sentences of Scripture for both Morning and Evening Prayer, after the word Scripture, as everyone can see by looking." He adds "This, however, is only a question of form, and ought not to interfere with the adoption of

been at last waived, a straight path is now open to the end desired, and it ought to be followed even at the cost of three years more of delay.

Returning to the general subject, and still following the order of the Table of Contents, we come to *Prayers and Thanksgivings upon several Occasions.*

Here it would be well to note more intelligibly than is done by the present rubric the proper places for the introduction of the Prayers and the Thanksgivings, providing for the use of the former before, and of the latter after the General Thanksgiving.

As to the deficiencies in this department let the late Dr. Muhlenberg speak.

"The Prayer Book," he says, "is not undervalued as to its treasures in asserting its wants. The latter cannot be denied. Witness the meagre amount of New Testament prayer and praise for the round of festivals and fasts; the absence of any forms suited to the peculiar circumstances of our own Church and country and to the times we live in; or for our benevolent and educational institutions. There are no prayers for the increase of Ministers, for Missions, or Missionaries, for the Christian teaching of the young; for sponsors on occasions of Baptism; for persons setting out on long journeys by land, quite as perilous as voyages by sea;

the amendment at the next Convention. It is to be hoped that the resolution for enrichment, so called, will present a variety of additions out of which an acceptable selection can be made, and when they are finally carried that the Book of Common Prayer will be not only the standard book, but a sealed book, so to speak, for as many generations as have passed since the present book was adopted."—Letter of the Hon. J. B. Howe of Indiana in *The Churchman* for January 29, 1881.

for the sick desiring the prayers of the Church when there is no prospect of or desire for recovery; for the bereaved at funerals, and many other occasions for which there might as well be provision as for those few for which we already have the occasional prayers."*

After the *Prayers and Thanksgivings* come *The Collects, Epistles, and Gospels.* Here again there is some room for enrichment. Distinctive collects for the first four days of Holy Week, for Monday and Tuesday in Easter Week, and for Monday and Tuesday in Whitsun Week, would add very materially to our liturgical wealth, while there would seem to be no reason whatever why they should not be had. It would also serve to enhance the symmetry of the Christian Year if the old feast of the Transfiguration† (August 6) were to be restored to its place among the recognized holydays of the Church and given its proper collect, epistle, and gospel.

There are some liturgists who desire the restoration of the introits of the First Book of Edward VI. The

---

* See page 578 of *Evangelical Catholic Papers.* A collection of Essays, Letters, and Tractates from Writings of Rev. Wm. Augustus Muhlenberg, D D., during the last forty years.

The failure of this devout and venerated man to secure sundry much desired liturgical improvements (although it yet remains to be seen whether the failure has been total) was perhaps due to a certain vagueness inherent in his plans of reform. A clear vision of the very thing desired seems to have been lacking, or at least the gift of imparting it to others. But even as no man has deserved better of the American Episcopal Church than he, so it is no more than right that his deeply cherished wishes should be had in careful remembrance.

† Now a "black-letter day" in the English Calendar.

introit (so called from being the psalm sung when the priest goes within the altar-rails) has been in modern usage replaced by a metrical hymn. A sufficient reason for not printing the introit for each day in full, just before the collect, as was the mode in Edward's Book, is that to do so would involve a costly sacrifice of room. A compromise course would be to insert between the title of each Sunday or holyday and the collect proper to it, a simple numerical reference stating whereabouts in the Psalter the introit for the day is to be found, and adding perhaps the Latin catchwords. Any attempt to make the use of the introit obligatory in our times would meet with deserved failure; the metrical hymn has gained too firm a hold upon the affections of the Church at large ever to be willingly surrendered.

Coming, next, to the orders for the administration of the two sacraments, we find ourselves on delicate ground, where serious change of any sort is out of the question. Permission, under certain circumstances, still further to abbreviate the Office of the Communion of the Sick might, however, be sought without giving reasonable cause of alarm to any, and general consent might perhaps also be had for a provision with respect to the Exhortation, "Dearly beloved in the Lord," that in "Churches where there is frequent Communion it shall suffice to read the Exhortation above written once in a month on the Lord's Day."*

There are three liturgical features of the Scottish Communion Office which some have thought might be advantageously transferred to our own service. They are (*a*) the inserting after Christ's summary of the Law

* The Convocation Prayer Book, *in loc.*

a response, *Lord, have mercy upon us and write these thy laws in our hearts, we beseech thee;* (*b*) the repeating by the people, after the reading of the Gospel, of a formula of thanks corresponding to the *Glory be to thee, O Lord,* that precedes it ; and (*c*) the saying or singing of an Offertory sentence at the presentation of the alms. Upon these suggested enrichments the present writer offers no opinion.

In the Order of Confirmation a substitution for the present preface * of a responsive opening, in which the bishop should charge the minister to present none but such as he has found by personal inquiry "apt and meet" for the reception of the rite would be a marked improvement.

The remaining Occasional Offices would seem to demand no change either in structure or contents, although in some, perhaps in all of them, additional rubrics would be helpful to worshippers.

Some addition to the number of Occasional Offices would be a real gain. We need, for instance, a short Office for the Burial of Infants and Young Children ; a Daybreak Office for Great Festivals ; an Office for Midday Prayer; an Office of Prayer in behalf of Missions and Missionaries ; an Office for the Setting apart of a Layman as a Reader, or as a Missionary ; a Form of Prayer at the Laying of a Corner-stone ; and possibly some others. It is evident that these new formularies might give opportunity for the introduction of hitherto unused collects, anthems, and benedictions of a sort that would greatly enhance the general usefulness of the Prayer Book.

* Originally only an explanatory rubric. See Procter, p. 397.

This completes the survey of the field of "liturgical enrichment." A full discussion of the allied topic, "flexibility of use," would involve the examination in detail of all the rubrics of the Prayer Book, and for this there is no room. It is enough to say that unless the rubrics, the hinges and joints of a service-book, are kept well oiled, much creaking is a necessary result. There are turning-points in our public worship where congregations almost invariably betray an awkward embarrassment, simply because there is nothing to tell them whether they are expected to stand or to sit or to kneel. It is easy to sneer at such points as trifles and to make sport of those who call attention to them; but if it is worth our while to have ritual worship at all it is also worth our while to make the directions as to how people are to behave adequate, explicit, plain. A lofty contempt for detail is not the token of good administration either in Church or State. To the list of defective rubrics add those that are confessedly obsolete and such as are palpably contradictory and we have a bill of particulars that would amply justify a rubrical revision of the Prayer Book even if nothing more were to be attempted.

There is another reason. Far more rapidly than many people imagine, we are drifting away from the position of a Church that worships by liturgy to that of a Church worshipping by directory. The multiplicity of "uses" that vexed the Anglican Reformers is in our day multiplied four-fold. To those who honestly consider a directory a better thing than a liturgy this process of relaxation is most welcome, but for others who hold that, until the binding clauses of a Book of Common Prayer have been formally rescinded, they ought to be observed, the spectacle is the reverse of edifying. They would much prefer seeing the channels of liberty opened at the touch of law, and this is one of their chief reasons for advocating revision.

Two questions remain untouched, both of them of great practical importance. Could the Prayer Book be enriched to the extent suggested in this paper without a serious and most undesirable increase in its bulk as a volume?

Even supposing this were possible, is it at all likely that the Church could be persuaded to accept the amended book?

Unless the first of these two eminently proper questions can be met, there is, or ought to be, an end to all talk about revision. The advantage to a Church of being able to keep all its authoritative formularies of worship within the compass of a single volume is inestimable. Even the present enforced severance of the Hymnal from the Prayer Book is a misfortune.*

Those were good days when "Bible and Prayer Book" was the Churchman's all sufficient formula so far as volumes were concerned.

Rome boasts a much larger ritual variety than ours, but she secures it by multiplying books. The Missal is in one volume, the Breviary in four, the Pontifical, the Ritual, and the Ceremonial in one each, making eight in all.† This is an evil, and one from which we Anglicans have had a happy escape. It was evidently with a

---

* Let us hope that before long there may be devised some better way of providing relief for our Widows and Orphans than that of the indirect taxation of the singers of hymns.

† The Greek Office Books, it is said, fill eighteen quartos.

great groan of relief that the Church of England shook herself free from the whole host of service-books, and established her one only volume. It behooves us to be watchful how we take a single step towards becoming entangled in the old meshes.*

But need the enrichment of the Prayer Book—such enrichment as has been described, necessarily involve an unwieldiness in the volume, or, what would be still worse, an overflow into a supplement? Certainly not; for by judicious management every change advocated in this paper, and more besides, might be accomplished without transgressing by so much as a page or a paragraph the limits of the present standard book. All the space needed could be secured by the simple expedient of omitting matter that has been found by actual experience to be superfluous. Redundancy and unnecessary repetition are to the discredit of a book that enjoys such an unrivalled reputation as the Common Prayer. They are blemishes upon the face of its literary perfectness. Who has not marvelled at the strange duplication of the Litany and the Office of the Holy Communion in the Ordinal, when the special petitions proper to those services when used in that connection might easily have been printed by themselves with a direction that they be inserted in the appointed place?

* In that naïve and racy bit of English (omitted in our American book) entitled *Concerning the Service of the Church*, one of the very choicest morsels is the following : " Moreover, the number and hardness of the Rules called the *Pie*, and the manifold changings of the Service, was the cause, that to turn the Book only was so hard and intricate a matter, that many times there was more business to find out what should be read than to read it when it was found out."

Scholars, of course, know perfectly well how this came about. The Ordinal does not belong to the Prayer Book proper, but has a separate identity of its own. When printed as a book by itself it is all very well that it should include the Litany and the Holy Communion in full, but why allow these superfluous pages to crowd out others that are really needed?*

It has already been explained how the room now occupied by the "Selections" might be economized, and by the same simple device the space engrossed by divers psalms here and there in the Occasional Offices, *e. g.*, Psalm li in the Visitation of Prisoners, and Psalm cxxx in the Visitation of the Sick could be made available for other use.

Again, why continue to devote a quarter of a page of precious space to the "Prayer for imprisoned debtors," seeing that now, for a long time past, there has been no such thing in the United States as imprisonment for debt? By availing ourselves of only a portion of these possible methods of garnering space, all that is desired

---

* It may be wise to buttress the position taken with a quotation out of Dr. Coit.

"We really, however, do not see any necessity for either of these Services in American Books, as with us the Ordinal always, *now*, makes a part of the Prayer Book in all editions. It would be a saving to expunge them and no change would be necessary, except the introduction of such a litanical petition and suffrage with the Services for Deacons and Priests, as already exists in the Service for Bishops. The Church of England retains the Litany in her Ordinal, for that, until latterly, was printed in a separate book, and was not to be had unless ordered expressly. And yet with even such a practice she has but one Communion Service. We study cheapness and expedition in our day. They can both be consulted here, *salva fide et salva ecclesia.*"—Report of 1844.

might be accomplished, without making the Prayer Book bulkier by a single leaf than it is to-day.

But would a Prayer Book thus enriched be accepted by the Church at large? Is there any reason to think that the inertia which inheres in all large bodies, and to a singularly marked degree in our own Communion, could be overcome? The General Convention can give an approximate answer to these questions; it cannot settle them decisively, for it is a body which mirrors only to a certain extent the real mind and temper of the constituencies represented in it. One thing is certain, that only by allowing fullest possible play to the principle of "local option" could any wholly new piece of work on the part of revisionists, however excellent it might be in itself considered, find acceptance. To allow features introduced into the body of an existing service to be accounted optional, would indeed be impossible, without gendering the very wildest confusion. Upon such points the Church would have to decide outright, for or against, and stand by her decisions. But as respects every additional and novel Office proposed, the greatest care ought to be taken to have the indefinite *An* rather than the definite *The* prefixed to it. Before such new uses are made binding on all, they must have met and endured the test of thorough trial by some. This is only fair.

But there is a limit, it must be remembered, in the Church's case to the binding power of precedent and prescription. The social order changes, and of these tides that ebb and flow it is our bounden duty to take note. Had mere aversion to change, dogged unwillingness to venture an experiment always carried the day, instead of having the "Prayer Book as it is," we should still be drearily debating the rival merits of Hereford and Sarum. The great question to be settled is, Does an emergency exist serious enough to warrant an attempt on our part to make better what we know already to be good? Is the Republic expecting of us, and reasonably expecting of us, greater things than with our present equipment we are quite able to accomplish? There are eyes that think they see a great future before this Church—are they right, or is it only mirage? At any rate ours is no return trip—we are outward bound. The ship is cutting new and untried waters with her keel at every moment. There is no occasion to question the sufficiency of either compass or helm, but in certain matters of a practical sort there is a demand upon us to use judgment, we are bound to give a place in our seamanship to present common-sense as well as to respect for ancient usage, and along with it all to feel some confidence that if the ship is what we think her to be, "the winds of God" may be trusted to bring her safely into port.

THE BOOK ANNEXED: ITS CRITICS AND ITS PROSPECTS.

THE BOOK ANNEXED: ITS CRITICS AND ITS PROSPECTS.*

I.

FIRST, last, and always this is to be said with respect to the revision of the American Common Prayer, that unless we can accomplish it with hearty good feeling the attempt at improvement ought to be abandoned altogether.

The day has gone by when new formularies of worship could be imposed on an unwilling Church by edict, and although under our carefully guarded system of ecclesiastical legislation there is little danger of either haste or unfairness, we must bear it well in mind that something more than "a constitutional majority of both houses" is needful if we would see liturgical revision crowned with real success. Of course, absolute unanimity is not to be expected. Every improvement that the world has seen was greeted at its birth by a chorus of select voices sounding the familiar anthem, "The old is better"; and the generation of those, who, in the sturdy phrase of King James's revisers, "give liking unto nothing but what is framed by themselves, and hammered on their anvil," will be always with us. But substantial unanimity may exist, even when absolute unanimity is impossible, and if anything like as gen-

* First printed in *The Church Review*, 1886.

eral a consent can be secured for revision in 1886 as was given to it in 1883, the friends of the movement will have good reason to be satisfied.

That there has been, since the publication of *The Book Annexed as Modified*, a certain measure of reaction against the spirit of change must be evident to all who watch carefully the pulse of public opinion in the Church. Whether this reaction be as serious as some imagine, whether it have good reasons to allege, and whether it be not already giving tokens of spent force, are points which in the present paper will be touched only incidentally, for the writer's purpose is rather irenic than polemical, and he is more concerned to remove misapprehensions and allay fears than to seek the fading leaf of a controversial victory.

LIMITATIONS.

No estimate of the merits and demerits of *The Book Annexed* can be a just one that leaves out of account the limitations under which the framers of it did their work. These limitations were not unreasonable ones. It was right and proper that they should be imposed. There is no good ground for a belief that the time will ever come when a "blank cheque," to borrow Mr. Goschen's mercantile figure, will be given to any company of liturgical revisers to fill out as they may see fit. But the moulders of forms, in whatever department of plastic art their specialty lies, when challenged to show cause why their work is deficient in symmetry or completeness, have an undoubted right to plead in reply the character of the conditions under which they labored. The present instance offers no exception to the general rule. In the first place, a distinct pledge was given in the House of Deputies, in 1880, before consent to the appointment of the Joint Committee was secured, that in case such permission to launch a movement in favor of revision as was asked for were to be granted, no attempt would be made seriously to change the Liturgy proper, namely, the Office of the Holy Communion.

The question was distinctly asked by a clerical deputy from the diocese of Maryland,* Do you desire to modify the Office of the Holy Communion? and it was as distinctly answered by the mover of the resolution under which the Joint Committee was finally appointed, No, we do not. It is true that such a pledge, made by a single member of one House, could only measurably control the action of a Joint Committee in which both Houses were to be represented; but it is equally plain that the maker of the pledge was in honor bound to do all in his power to secure the observance of its terms.

Let this historical fact be noted by those who are disposed to complain that the Joint Committee did not pull to pieces and entirely rearrange the Anglo-Scoto-American Office, which now for a long time, and until quite recently, we have been taught to esteem the nearest possible approach to liturgical perfection.

Under this same head of "limitations" must be set down the following resolutions passed by the Joint Committee itself, at its first regular meeting:

Resolved, That this Committee asserts, at the outset, its conviction that no alteration should be made touching either statements or standards of doctrine in the Book of Common Prayer.

* The Rev. Dr. Orlando Hutton.

Resolved, That this Committee, in all its suggestions and acts, be guided by those principles of liturgical construction and ritual use which have guided the compilation and amendments of the Book of Common Prayer, and have made it what it is.

It was manifestly impossible, under resolutions like these, to depart very widely from established precedent, or in any serious measure to disturb the foundations of things.

The first of them shut out wholly the consideration of such questions as the reinstatement of the Athanasian Creed or the proposal to make optional the use of the word " regenerate " in the Baptismal Offices ; while the other forbade the introduction of such sentimental and grotesque conceits as " An Office for the Blessing of Candles," " An Office for the Benediction of a Lifeboat," and " An Office for the Reconciliation of a Lapsed Cleric." *

Still another very serious limitation, and one especially unfriendly to that perfectness of contour which we naturally look to see in a liturgical formulary, grew out of the tender solicitude of the Committee for what may be called the vested rights of congregations. There was a strong reluctance to the cutting away even of what might seem to be dead wood, lest there should ensue, or be thought to ensue, the loss of something really valuable.

It was only as the result of much painstaking effort, and only at some sacrifice of literary fastidiousness, that the Committee was enabled to report a book of which it could be said that, while it added much of possible enrichment, it took away almost nothing that had been

*_Priest's Prayer Book_, Fifth edition, pp. 238, 243, 281.

in actual possession.* There could be no better illustration of this point than is afforded by certain of the alterations proposed to be made in the Order for Evening Prayer.

The Committee felt assured that upon no point was the judgment of the Church likely to be more unanimous than in approving the restoration to their time-honored home in the Evening Office of *Magnificat* and *Nunc dimittis*, and yet so unwilling were they to displace *Bonum est confiteri* and *Benedic anima mea* from positions they have only occupied since 1789 that they authorized the unquestionably clumsy expedient of printing three responds to each Lesson.

Probably a large majority of the Committee would have preferred to drop *Bonum est confiteri* and *Benedic anima mea* altogether, retaining *Cantate Domino* and *Deus misereatur* as the sole alternates to the two Gospel canticles, as in the English Book, but rather than have a thousand voices cry out, as it was believed they would cry out, "You have robbed us," the device of a second alternate was adopted, to the sad defacement of the printed page. In may be charged that, in thus choosing, the Committee betrayed timidity, and that a wise boldness would have been the better course; but if account be taken of the attitude consistently maintained by General Convention towards any proposition for the change of so much as a comma in the Prayer Book, during a period of fifty years prior to the introduction of *The Book Annexed*, it will perhaps be concluded that for the characterization of the Com-

* The *Prayer for Imprisoned Debtors* is believed to be the only formulary actually dropped.

mittee's policy timidity is scarcely so proper a word as caution.

SPECIAL CRITICISMS.

(a) Foreign.

As there is reason to believe that opinion at home has been very considerably affected by foreign criticism of *The Book Annexed*, it will be well at this point to give some attention to what has been said in English journals in review of the work thus far accomplished. The more noteworthy of the foreign criticisms are those contained in *The Church Quarterly Review*, *The Church Times*, and *The Guardian*.*

The Church Quarterly reviewer opens with an expression of deep regret at " the failure to take advantage of the opportunity for reinstating the Athanasian Creed." As already observed, no such opportunity existed. By formal vote the Joint Committee debarred itself from any proceeding of this sort, and the Convention, which sat in judgment on its work, was manifestly of opinion that in so acting the Committee had rightly interpreted its charter.

The reviewer, who is in full sympathy with the movement for enrichment as such, goes on to recommend, as a more excellent way than that followed in *The Book Annexed*, the compilation of

An Appendix to the Book of Common Prayer to contain the much needed *Additional Services* for both Sunday and other use in churches, in mission chapels, and in religious communities, as

* *The Church Quarterly Review* for April, 1884, and July, 1884. *The Church Times* for August 29, 1884; also July 31, August 7, 14, 21, 28, September 4, 1885. *The Guardian* for July 20, 1885.

well as a full supply of *Occasional Prayers and Thanksgivings* for objects and purposes, missionary and otherwise, which are as yet entirely unrepresented in our Offices.

There are obvious reasons why this device should commend itself to an English Churchman, for it is unlikely that anything better than this, or, indeed, anything one half so satisfactory, could be secured by Act of Parliament.

For something very much better than this, however, a self-governed Church, like our own, has a right to look, and, in all probability, will continue to look until the thing is found. An *Appendix* to a manual of worship, whether the manual be Prayer Book or Hymnal,* is and cannot but be, from the very nature of things, a blemish to the eye, an embarrassment to the hand, and a vexation to the spirit. Such *addenda* carry on their face the suggestion that they are makeshifts, postscripts, after-thoughts; and in their lack of dignity, as well as of convenience, pronounce their own condemnation.

Moreover, in our particular case, no "Appendix," "Prymer," or "Authorized Vade-mecum" could accomplish the ends that are most of all desired. Fancy putting the *Magnificat*, the *Nunc dimittis*, the Versicles that follow the Creed, and the "Lighten our darkness" into an "Appendix." It would be the defeat of our main object.

Then, too, this is to be remembered, that in order to secure a "fully authorized Appendix," we, in this country, should be obliged to follow precisely the same legal process we follow in altering the Prayer Book. If an Occasional Office cannot pass the ordeal of the criticism

* Recall the "Additional Hymns" of 1868.

of two successive Conventions, it ought not to be set forth at all; if it can and does stand that test, then it ought to be inserted in the Prayer Book in the particular place where it most appropriately belongs and may most readily be found.

Moreover, it should be remembered that one, and by no means the least efficient, of the causes that brought the Common Prayer into existence in the sixteenth century was disgust at the multiplication of service-books. We American Churchmen have two already; let us beware of adding a third.

The critic of *The Quarterly* was probably unacquainted with the fact that in the American Episcopal Church the experimental setting forth of Offices "for optional and discretional use" is not possible under the terms of the Constitution. We either must adopt outright and for permanent use, or else peremptorily reject whatever is urged upon us in the name of liturgical improvement.

Entering next upon a detailed criticism of the contents of *The Book Annexed* the writer proceeds to offer a number of suggestions, some of them of great value. He pleads earnestly and with real force for the restoration of the Lord's Prayer to its "place of honor" between the Creed and the Preces, showing, in a passage of singular beauty, how the whole daily office "may be said to have grown out of, or radiated from, or been crystallized round the central *Pater noster*," even as "from the Words of Institution has grown the Christian Liturgy."

The critic has only praise for the amendments in the Office for Thanksgiving Day; approves the selection of Proper Sentences for the opening of Morning and Evening Prayer; avers, certainly with truth, that the Office of the Beatitudes might be improved; welcomes "the very full repertory of special prayers"; thinks that the *Short Office of Prayer for Sundry Occasions* "certainly supplies a want"; rejoices in the recognition of the Feast of the Transfiguration; and closes what is by far the most considerable, and, both as respects praise and blame, the most valuable of all the reviews that have been made of *The Book Annexed* whether at home or abroad, with these words :

On the whole, we very heartily congratulate our Transatlantic brothers on the labors of their Joint Committee. We hope their recommendations may be adopted, and more in the same direction ; and that the two or three serious blemishes which we have felt constrained to point out and to lament may be removed from the book in the form finally adopted

And further, we very earnestly trust that this work, which has been very evidently so carefully and conscientiously done, may speedily, by way of example and precedent, bear fruit in a like process of enrichment among ourselves.

Commending these last words to the consideration of those who take alarm at the suggestion of touching the Prayer Book lest we may hurt the susceptibilities of our "kin beyond sea," and unduly anticipate that "joint action of both Churches," which, at least until disestablishment comes, must always remain a sheer impossibility, we pass to a consideration of the six articles contributed to the *Church Times* in July and August last, under the title, *The Revised American Prayer Book*. Here we come upon a writer who, if not always edifying, has the undoubted merit of being never dull. In fact, so deliciously are logical inconsequence and accidental humor mingled throughout his fifteen columns of discursive criticism that a suspicion arises as to the writer's nationality. It is doubtful whether anyone born on the English side of the Irish Sea could possibly have suggested the establishment of a Saint's Day in honor of the late respected Warden of Racine College, or seriously have proposed that Messrs. Oliver Wendell Holmes, Russell Lowell, Henry James, and W. D. Howells be appointed a jury of "literary arbitrament" to sit in judgment on the liturgical language of *The Book Annexed;* and this out of respect to our proper national pride. Doubtless it would add perceptibly to the amused sense of the unfitness of things with which these eminent liberals must have seen themselves thus named, if permission could be given to the jury, when empanelled, to "co-opt" into its number Mr. Samuel Clemens and Mr. Dudley Warner.*

The general tenor of the writer in *The Church Times* may fairly be inferred from the following extract from the first article of the series :

The judgment that must be pronounced on the work as a whole is precisely that which has been passed on the Revised

---

* This proposal of arbitration has occasioned so much innocent mirth that, in justice to the maker of it, attention should be called to the ambiguity of the language in which it is couched. The wording of the passage is vague. It is just possible that by "the question ",which he would be content to submit to the judgment of the four specified men of letters, he means, not, as he has been understood to mean, the whole subject-matter of *The Book Annexed*, but only the abstract question whether verbal variations from the English original of the Common Prayer be or be not, on grounds of purity of style, desirable Even if this be all that he means there is perhaps still room for a smile, but, at all events, he ought to have the benefit of the doubt,

New Testament, that there are doubtless some few changes for the better, so obvious and so demanded beforehand by all educated opinion that to have neglected them would at once have stamped the revisers as blockheads and dunces ; but that the set-off in the way of petty and meddlesome changes for the worse, neglect of really desirable improvements, bad English, failure in the very matter of pure scholarship just where it was least to be expected, and general departure from the terms of the Commission assigned to them (notably by their introduction of confusion instead of flexibility into the services, so that the congregation can seldom know what is going to happen) has so entirely outweighed the merits of the work that it cannot possibly be adopted by the Church, and must be dismissed as a dismal fiasco, to be dealt with anew in some more adequate fashion

This paragraph is not reproduced for the purpose of discrediting the writer of it as a judge of English prose, for there are various passages in the course of the six articles that would more readily lend themselves to such a use. The object in quoting it is simply to put the reader into possession, in a compact form, of the most angry, even if not the most formidable, of the various indictments yet brought against *The Book Annexed*.

Moreover, the last words of the extract supply a good text for certain didactic remarks that ought to be made, with respect to what is possible and what is not possible in the line of liturgical revision in America.

Worthless as the result of the Joint Committee's labors has turned out to be, their motive, we are assured, was a good one. The critic's contention is not that the work they undertook is a work that ought not to be done, but rather that when done it should be better done. The revision as presented must be " dismissed as a dismal fiasco," but only dismissed " in order to be dealt with anew in some more adequate fashion." But on what ground can we rest this sanguine expectation of better things to come? Whence is to originate and how is to be appointed the commission of "experts" which is to give us at last the "Ideal Liturgy"?

Cardinal Newman in one of his lesser controversial tracts remarks:

> If the English people lodge power in the many, not in the few, what wonder that its operation is roundabout, clumsy, slow, intermittent, and disappointing? You cannot eat your cake and have it; you cannot be at once a self-governing nation and have a strong government.*

Similarly it may be said that, however great the difficulties that beset liturgical revision by legislative process at the hands of some five hundred men, nevertheless the fact remains that the body known in law as The Protestant Episcopal Church in the United States of America has provided in its Constitution that change in its formularies shall be so effected and not otherwise. It may turn out that we must give up in despair the whole movement for a better adaptation of our manual of worship to the needs of our land and of our time; it may be found that the obstacles in the way are absolutely insuperable; but let us dream no dreams of seeing this thing handed over, "with power," to a "commission of experts," for that is something which will never come to pass.

Whether "experts" in liturgics are any more likely to furnish us with good prayers than "experts" in prosody are likely to give us the best poetry is a tempting question, but one that must be left, for the present, on one side. Perhaps, if the inquiry were to be pushed, we

---

* *Discussions and Arguments*, p. 341.

might find ourselves shut up to the curious conclusion that the framers of the very earliest liturgies, the authors of the old sacramentaries, were either verbally inspired or else were lacking in the qualifications which alone could fit them to do worthily the work they worthily did, for clearly " experts " they were not.

But the question that immediately concerns us is one of simple fact. Assuming the present laborious effort at betterment to have been proved a "fiasco," how is the General Convention to set in motion any more promising enginery of revision? "Summon in," say our English advisers, "competent scholars, and give them *carte blanche* to do what they will." But the Convention, which is by law the final arbiter, has no power to invite to a share in its councils men who have no constitutional right to a seat upon its floor. How thankfully should we welcome as participants in our debates and as allies in our legislation the eminent liturgical scholars who give lustre to the clergy list of the Church of England ; but we are as powerless to make them members of the General Convention as we should be to force them into the House of Commons. The same holds true at home. If the several dioceses fail to discover their own " inglorious Miltons," and will not send them up to General Convention, General Convention may, and doubtless does, lament the blindness of the constituencies, but it cannot correct their blunder. The dioceses in which the "experts" canonically reside had had full warning that important liturgical interests were to be discussed and acted upon in the General Convention of 1883 ; why were the "experts" left at home? And if they were not returned in 1883, is there sufficient reason to believe that they will ever be returned in any coming year of grace? It must be either that the American Church is bereft of "experts," or else that the constituencies, influenced possibly by the hard sense of the laity, have learned hopelessly to confound the "expert" with the doctrinaire.

Of "expert testimony," in the shape of the liturgical material gathered, mainly by English writers, during the last fifty years, the Joint Committee had no lack. That this material was carefully sifted and conscientiously used, *The Book Annexed* will itself one day be acknowledged to be the sufficient evidence.

There is still another point that must be taken into account in this connection, to wit, the attitude which the Episcopate has a right to take with respect to any proposed work of liturgical revision. Bishops have probably become inured to the hard measure habitually dealt out to them in the columns of the *Church Times*, and are unlikely to allow charges of ignorance and incompetency so far to disturb their composure as to make them afraid to prosecute a work which, from time immemorial, has been held to lie peculiarly within their province. It may be affirmed, with some confidence, that no revision of the American Offices will ever be ratified, in the conduct of which the Bishops of the Church have not been allowed the leadership which belongs to them of right. Then it is for the General Convention carefully to consider whether any House of Bishops destined to be convened in our time is likely to have on its roll the names of any prelates more competent, whether on the score of learning or of practical experience, to deal with a work of liturgical revision than were the seven prelates elected by the free voice of their brethren to represent the Episcopal Order on the Joint Committee of Twenty-one.

Coming to details the reviewer of the *Church Times* regrets, first of all, the failure of the Convention to change the name of the Church. He goes on to express a disapproval, more or less qualified, of the discretionary power given to bishops to set forth forms of prayer for special occasions, and of the continued permission to use Selections of Psalms instead of the psalms for the day. It is not quite clear whether he approves the expansion of the Table of Proper Psalms or not, though he thinks it "abstractedly desirable" that provision be made in this connection for "Corpus Christi and All Souls."

He condemns the latitude allowed in the choice of lessons under the rules of the new lectionary, fearing that a clergyman who happens to dislike any given chapter because of its contents may be tempted habitually to suppress it by substituting another, but in the very next paragraph he gravely questions the expediency of limiting congregations to such hymns as have been "duly set forth and allowed by authority." Yet most observers, at least on this side of the water, are of opinion that liberty of choice within the limits of the Bible is a far safer freedom, so far as the breeding of heresy goes, than liberty of choice beyond the limits of the Hymnal has proved itself to be. The reviewer is pleased with the addition of the Feast of the Transfiguration to the Calendar, but "desiderates more," and would gladly welcome the introduction into the Prayer Book of commemorations of eminent saints, from Ignatius down,* but of this, mention has already been made, and it is unnecessary to revert to it.

There follows next a protest against the selection of proper Sentences prefixed to Morning and Evening Prayer.

> The revisers seem to have a glimmering of what was the right thing to do, . . . but they should have swept away the undevotional and unliturgical plan of beginning with certain detached texts, which has no fitness whatever, and has never even seemed to answer any useful end.

This is stronger language than most of us are likely to approve. A Church that directly takes issue with Rome, as ours does, with respect to the true source of authority in religion has an excellent reason for letting the voice of Holy Scripture sound the key-note of her daily worship, whether there be ancient precedent for such a use or not. At the same time, the reviewer's averment that "the only proper opening is the Invocation of the Holy Trinity" is entitled to attention; and it is worth considering whether the latter portion of the nineteenth verse of the twenty-eighth chapter of St. Matthew's Gospel might not be advantageously added to the list of opening Sentences, for optional use.

In speaking of the new alternate to the Declaration of Absolution, the reviewer suggests most happily that it would be well to revive the form of mutual confession of priest and people found in the old service-books.†

---

* "The list might be brought down as late as the authorities pleased to bring it, even to include, if they chose, such names as John Keble, James De Koven, and Ferdinand Ewer."—*The Church Times* for August 14, 1885.

† This form of absolution suggested as an alternate in *The Book Annexed* is taken from the source mentioned.

This proposal would probably not be entertained in connection with the regular Orders for Morning and Evening Prayer, but room for such a feature might perhaps be found in some optional office.

After a grudging commendation of the steps taken in *The Book Annexed* to restore the Gospel Canticles, the reviewer next puts in a strong plea for a larger allowance of versicles and responses after the Creed, contending that this is "just one of the places where enrichment, much beyond that of replacing the English versicles and responses now missing, is feasible and easy," to which the answer is that we, who love these missing versicles, shall think ourselves fortunate if we succeed in regaining only so much as we have lost. Even this will be accomplished with difficulty. It is most interesting, however, to notice that this stout defender of all that is English acknowledges the coupling together of the versicle, "Give peace in our time, O Lord," and the response, "Because there is none other that fighteth for us, but only thou, O God," to be "a very infelicitous *non-sequitur*." For correcting this palpable incongruity, the authors of *The Book Annexed* have been sharply criticised here at home. What were they that they should have presumed to disturb ancient Anglican precedent in such a point? If we could not understand why the God of battles, as the God of battles, should be implored to "give peace in our time," so much the worse for our intelligence. But here comes the most acrid of all our critics, and shows how the collocation of sentences in the English Book has, from the beginning, been due to a palpable blunder in condensing an office of the Sarum Breviary. Of the American substitute for this "unhappy response" the best he can say, however, is that it is "well intentioned."

Of the "Office of the Beatitudes" the reviewer declares that it "needs thorough recasting before it can stand," and in this we agree with him, as will hereafter appear, though wholly unable to concur in his sweeping condemnation, in this connection, of one of the most beautiful of Canon Bright's liturgical compositions, the Collect beginning, "O God, by whom the meek are guided in judgment and light riseth up in darkness for the godly." Of this exquisite piece of idiomatic English, the reviewer allows himself to speak as being "a very poor composition, defective in rhythm."

The criticism of the eucharistic portions of *The Book Annexed* is mainly in the line of complaint that more has not been added in the way of new collects and proper prefaces, but upon this point it is unnecessary to dwell, the reasons having been already given why the Joint Committee and the Convention left the liturgy proper almost untouched. Neither is there anything that specially calls for notice or serious reply in what is said about the Occasional Offices.

The Office for the Burial of Children is acknowledged to be a needed addition, but as it stands "is pitched in an entirely wrong key. The cognate offices in the *Rituale Romanun* and the *Priest's Prayer Book* ought to have shown the Committee, were it not for their peculiar unteachableness, a better way." To one who can read between the lines, this arraignment of the Americans for their lack of docility to the teachings of the *Priest's Prayer Book* is not devoid of drollery.

It will happily illustrate the peculiar difficulties that

beset liturgical revision to close this *résumé* of the censures of *The Church Times* by printing, side by side, the reviewer's estimate of the changes proposed in the Confirmation Office and the independent judgment of a learned evangelical divine of our own Church upon the same point.

The Confirmation Service, as one of the very poorest in the Anglican rites, stood particularly in need of amendment and enrichment, especially by the removal of the ambiguous word "confirm" applied to the acts of the candidates, whereby the erroneous opinion that they came merely to confirm and ratify their baptismal promises, and not to be confirmed and strengthened in virtue of something bestowed upon them, has gained currency.

Thus far the English Ritualist. Here follows the American Evangelical:

I still hope you will see your way clear to modify the present draft of the proposed Confirmation Office, as it gives a much higher Sacramentarian idea of it than the present, a concession which will greatly please the Sacerdotalists, to which they are by no means entitled.

The critic of *The Guardian* is a writer of different make, and entitled every way to the most respectful attention. His fault-finding, which is invariably courteous, is mainly confined to the deficiencies of *The Book Annexed*.

He would have had more done rather than less; but at the same time clearly points out that under the restrictions which controlled the Committee more could not fairly have been expected. He regrets that in restoring the lost portions of *Venite* and *Benedictus* the Convention did not make the use of the complete form in every case obligatory; and of the eight concluding verses of the latter canticle, which under the rubric of *The Book Annexed* are only obligatory during Advent, he says, "Imagine their omission on Christmas Day!"

To this criticism there are several answers, any one of which may be held to be sufficient. In the first place, it should be remembered that into the Committee's plan of enrichment there entered the element of differentiation. The closing portion of the *Venite* has a special appropriateness to Lent; the closing portion of the *Benedictus* a special appropriateness to Advent. Moreover, if any congregations desire the whole of these two canticles throughout the year, there is nothing in the rubrics of *The Book Annexed* to forbid such an enjoyment of them. They *may* be sung in full always; but only in Lent in the one case, and in Advent in the other, *must* they be so sung. The revision Committee was informed, on what was considered the highest authority, that in the Church of England the *Benedictus*, on account of its length, had been very generally disused. But, however this may be, there can be little doubt that the effort after restoration would have failed completely in the late Convention had the use of these two canticles in full been insisted upon by the promoters of revision.

There is less of verbal criticism in *The Guardian's* review than could have been wished, for any suggestions with respect to inaccuracies of style or rhythmical shortcomings would have been most welcome from the pen of so competent a censor. Attention is called to the unmusical flow of language in the alternate Confession provided for the Evening Office; the figurative features of the proposed Collect for Maundy-Thursday are characterized as infelicitous; and the Collect provided for the Feast of the Transfiguration is declared to be inferior to the corresponding one in the Sarum Breviary.

Of this sort of criticism, at the hands of men who know their craft, *The Book Annexed* cannot have too much. In fact, of such immeasurable importance is good English in this connection, that it would be no hardship were every separate clause of whatever formulary it may be proposed to engraft upon the Prayer Book to be subjected to the most searching tests.

Let an epoch be agreed upon, if necessary, that shall serve as the criterion of admissibility for words and phrases. Let it be decided, for instance, that no word that cannot prove an Elizabethan parentage, or, if this be too severe a standard, then no word of post-Caroline origin, shall be admitted within the sacred precincts. Probably there are words in *The Book Annexed* which such a canon would eject; but let us have them pointed out, and their merits and demerits discussed. Such criticism would be of infinitely more value to the real interests of revision than those vague and general charges of "crudeness" and "want of finish" which it is always so easy to make and sometimes so difficult to illustrate.

The writer in *The Guardian* closes an only too brief commentary upon what the Convention has laid before the Church with the following words:

Many of the proposals now in question are excellent, but others will be improved by reconsideration in the light of fuller ritual study, such as will be seen to produce a more exact and cultured ritual αἰσθησις, perhaps we may, without offence, add, a more delicate appreciation of rhythm. What *The Book Annexed* presents to us in the way of emendation is, on the whole, good ; but, if subjected to a deliberate recension, it would, we predict, become still better. If thus improved by the Convention of 1886, it might be finally adopted by the Convention of 1889.

This conspectus of English critical opinion would be incomplete were no account to be made of the utterances of the various writers and speakers who dealt with the general subject of liturgical revision at the recent Church Congress at Portsmouth.

The Book Annexed could scarcely ask a more complete justification than is supplied by these testimonies of men who at least may be supposed to be acquainted with the needs of the Church of England.

The following catena, made up from three of the four papers* read upon the Prayer Book, gives a fair notion of the general tone of the discussion. It will be worth anyone's while to collate it with the thirty Resolutions that make up the " Notification to the Dioceses."

> Can it be seriously doubted that there are requirements of this age which are not satisfied by the provision for public worship made in the sixteenth century ? Can any really suppose that the compilers of that brief manual, the Prayer Book, however proud we may rightly be of their work, were so gifted with inspired foresight as to save the Church of future ages the responsibilities of considering and supplying the devotional wants of successive generations?
>
> Who has not felt the scantiness of holy association in our Sunday and week-day worship ? . . . Much, I know, has been

---

* The paper read by the Dean of Worcester dealt exclusively with the legal aspects of the question as it concerns the Church of England.

supplied by our hymnology, which has progressed nobly in proportion as the meagreness of our liturgical provision has been realized. But beyond hymns we need actual forms of service, which shall strike the ear and touch the heart by fresh and vivid adaptations of God's Word to the great mysteries of the Gospel faith. . . After-services on Sunday evenings have of late grown common; for them we need also the aid of regular and elastic forms

Most deplorably have we felt the need of intercessory services for Home and Foreign Missions; and, though there are beautiful metrical litanies which bear directly on these and other objects, yet these are not sufficient, and of course are limited to times when a good and strong choir can be secured; . . . and further we want very simple forms of prayer to accompany addresses given in homes and mission rooms.*

I declare it as my conviction, after many years of (I hope) a not indolent ministry, and of many opportunities of observation and experiment, that the Church stands in pressing and immediate need of a few rearrangements and adaptations of some of her Offices; also of an enormous number of supplementary Offices or services—some for frequent use, others for occasional purposes within the consecrated buildings; and that besides these there is need of a supply of special Offices for the use of a recognized lay agency outside of the church edifices

Why limit our introductory sentences to seven deprecatory texts? . . . Why can we not introduce the anthem used on Easter-day, instead of the *Venite*, throughout the Octave, or at least on Easter Monday and Tuesday? Would not spiritual life be deepened and intensified, and, best of all, be strengthened, by the use in the same manner of a suitable anthem instead of the *Venite* on Advent Sundays, on Christmas-day, at Epiphany, on Ash-Wednesday, on Good Friday, during Rogation days, at Ascension-tide, and on harvest festivals and the special annual Church festival of the year?

* The Rev. Edgar Morris Dumbleton (Rector of St James's, Exeter)

I submit that an enrichment of the Book of Common Prayer is also required. For although, as already suggested, this may be provided to some extent by a Collect for occasional use before the final prayer of Morning Prayer or Evensong, the needs of the Church will not be fully supplied without some complete additional offices. Certainly an additional service for Sunday afternoon and evening. . . The times are very solemn, and we must wait no longer. . . We have talked for nearly twenty-five years—not vainly, I believe—but let us "go and do" not a little in the next five years. . . Prove yourself to be of the Church of God by doing all the work of the Church, and in the proper way Proclaim before our God by your actions and your activities, and by providing all that is needed, not only for Churchmen, but for earnest Christians who are not Churchmen, and for the poor, weary sinners who are living as if there were neither Church nor Saviour, such services for the one, and such means for drawing the others to Christ, that they all may become one in him. And for all this you must have (as I think):

1. Possibly a small rearrangement of existing services.
2. Variety and additions in some of these services.
3. Enrichment by many services supplementary.
4. Services for use by laymen.

I wish to alarm none, but I wish we were all astir, for there is no time to wait.*

I should like to suggest, if it seems desirable, as it does to me, to make any further variation from the original arrangement of Morning Prayer, that on such days as Easter-day, Whitsunday, and Ascension-day we should begin in a little different fashion than we do now.

Is it always needful to begin on such great days of rejoicing for Christians with the *same* sentences and the *same* Exhortation and Confession, and have to wait, so to speak, to give vent to our feelings till we reach the special psalms for the day? Might we not on such days accept the glorious facts, and begin with some

---

*The Rev. George Venables (Hon. Canon of Norwich and Vicar of Great Yarmouth).

special and appropriate psalm or anthem? . . . Thus we should at once get the great doctrine of the day, and be let to rejoice in it at the very outset, and then go on to the LORD's Prayer and the rest as we have it now. Confession of sin and absolution are not left out in the services of the day, as, of course, they occur in the Holy Communion; but leaving them out in the ordinary services, and beginning in the way suggested, would at one and the same time mark the day more clearly, and give opportunity for Christian gladness to show itself. . . Only one other alteration would, I think, be needed, namely, that a good selection of psalms be made, and used, as in the American Church, at the discretion of the minister I think all must feel that for one reason or another all the psalms are not adapted for the ordinary worship of a mixed congregation, and this plan would ease the minds of many clergy and laity. Also copying the American Church, it would be well to omit the Litany on Christmas-day, Easter-day, and Whitsunday.*

In the light of this summary of Anglican *desiderata*, compiled by wholly friendly hands, it is plain that whatever we may do in this country in the line of liturgical revision, always supposing it to be gravely and carefully done, instead of harming, ought marvellously to help the real interests of the Church of England. Certain principles of polity adopted in our own Church a century ago, and notably among them those affecting the legislative rights of the laity in matters ecclesiastical, are beginning to find tardy recognition in the England of the present. Possibly a hundred years hence, or sooner, a like change of mind may bring English Churchmen to the approval of liturgical methods which, even if not wholly consonant to the temper of the Act of Uniformity, have nevertheless been found useful and effective in the work of bringing the truth and the power of God

* The Rev. Arthur James Robinson (Rector of Whitechapel).

to bear upon the common life of a great nation. The Church of England is to-day moving on toward changes and chances of which she sees enough already to alarm and not yet enough to reassure her. The dimness of uncertainty covers what may yet turn out to be the Mount of her Transfiguration, and she fears as she enters into the cloud. How shall we best and most wisely show our sympathy? By passing resolutions of condolence? By childish commiseration, the utterance of feigned lips, upon the approaching sorrows of disestablishment? Not thus at all, but rather by a courageous and well-considered pioneering work, which shall have it for its purpose to feel the ground and blaze the path which presently she and we may find ourselves treading in company. Tied as she is, for her an undertaking of this sort is impossible. We can show her no greater kindness than by entering upon it of our own motion and alone.

(b) *American.*

Criticism at home has been abundant; much of it intelligent and helpful, and by no means so much of it as might have been expected captious. Of what may be called official reviews there have been three, one from the Diocese of Central New York, one from the Diocese of Wisconsin, and one from the Diocese of Easton. The subject has also been dealt with in carefully prepared essays published from time to time in *The Church Review* and *The Church Eclectic,* while in the case of the weekly journals the treatment of the topic has been so frequent and so full that a mere catalogue of the editorial articles and contributed communications in which, during the two years last past, liturgical revision has been discussed would overtax the limits of the present paper.

The only practicable means of dealing with this mass of criticism is to adopt the inductive method, and to seek to draw out from the utterances of these many voices the four or five distinct concepts that severally lie behind them.

In limine, however, let this be said, that the broadest generalization of all is one to which the very discordance of the critics bears the best possible witness. Of a scheme of revision against which is pressed, in Virginia,* the charge of Mariolatry; in Ohio,† the charge of Latitudinarianism; and in Wisconsin,‡ the charge of Puritanic pravity, this much may at least be said, that it possesses the note of fairness. From henceforth suggestions of partisan bias are clearly out of order.

The Anglo-Catholic censures of *The Book Annexed* are substantially summed up in the assertion that due regard is not had, in the changes proposed, to the structural principles of liturgical science. In the exceedingly well written, if somewhat one-sided document, already referred to as the Wisconsin Report, this is, throughout, the burden of the complaint. The accomplished author of the Report, than whom no one of the critics at home or abroad has shown a keener or a better

---

* See letter of "J. L W." in *The Southern Churchman* for August 6, 1885

† See letter of "Ritualist" in *The Standard of the Cross* for July 2, 1885

‡ See the "Report of the Committee of the Council of the Diocese of Wisconsin," *passim*.

cultivated liturgical instinct, is afraid that a free use of all the liberties permitted by the new rubrics of the daily offices would so revolutionize Morning and Evening Prayer as practically to obliterate the line of their descent from the old monastic forms. If there were valid ground for such an expectation the alarm might be justifiable; but is there? The practical effect of the rubrics that make for abbreviation will be to give us back, on weekdays almost exactly, and with measurable precision on Sundays also, the Matins and Evensong of the First Book of Edward VI. Surely this is not the destruction of continuity with the pre-Reformation Church.

In his dislike of the provision for grafting the Beatitudes upon the Evening Prayer, the author of the Wisconsin Report will have many sympathizers, the present writer among them; but in his fear that in the introduction of the Proem to the Song of the Three Children, as a possible respond to the First Lesson,* there lurks a covert design to dethrone the *Te Deum*, he is likely to find few to agree with him.

But after all, may not this scrupulous regard for the precedents set us in the old service-books be carried too

---

* The evident intention of the Joint Committee in the introduction of this Canticle was to make it possible to shorten the Morning Prayer on week-days, without spoiling the structure of the office, as is now often done, by leaving out one of the Lessons. It is certainly open to question whether a better alternate might not have been provided, but it is surprising to find so well furnished a scholar as the Wisconsin critic speaking of the *Benedictus es Domine* as a liturgical novelty, "derived neither from the Anglican or the more ancient service-books." As a matter of fact the *Benedictus es Domine* was sung daily in the Ambrosian Rite at Matins, and is found also in the Mozarabic Breviary.

far? It is wholesome, but there is a limit to the wholesomeness of it. We remember who it was that made war for the sake of "a scientific frontier." Some of the scientific frontiers in the region of liturgics are as illusory as his was. For example, *The Book Annexed* may be "unscientific" in drawing as largely as it does on the language of the Apocalypse for versicles and responses. There has certainly been a departure from Anglican precedent in this regard. And yet it would scarcely seem that we could go far astray in borrowing from the liturgy of heaven, whether there be earthly precedent or not.

Cranmer and his associates made a far bolder break with the old office-books than *The Book Annexed* makes with the Standard Common Prayer. The statement of the Wisconsin Report, that "The Reformers of the English Church did not venture to write new Offices of Prayer," must be taken with qualifications. They did not make offices absolutely *de novo*, but they did condense and combine old offices in a manner that practically made a new thing of them. They took the monastic services and courageously remoulded them into a form suitable for the new era in which monasteries were to exist no longer.

Happily they were so thorough in their work that comparatively little change is called for in adapting what they fitted to the needs of the sixteenth century to the more varied requirements of the nineteenth. Still, when they are quoted as conservatives, and we are referred for evidence of their dislike of change to that particular paragraph of the Preface to the English Prayer Book entitled, *Concerning the Service of the*

Church,* it is worth our while to follow up the reference and see what is actually there said. The Wisconsin Committee use very soft words in speaking of the mediæval perversions and corruptions of Divine Service. "It was in the monasteries chiefly," they tell us, "that these services received the embellishments and wonderful variety which we find in the later centuries." But the following is the cruel manner in which, in the English Preface cited as authority, the "embellishments" and "wonderful variety" are characterized:

> But these many years past, this godly and ancient order of the ancient fathers hath been so altered, broken, and neglected, by planting in uncertain stories and legends, with multitudes of responds, verses, vain repetitions, commemorations, and synodals, that commonly when any book of the Bible was begun, after three or four chapters were read out, all the rest were unread.
> . . . And furthermore, notwithstanding that the ancient fathers have divided the Psalms into seven portions, whereof every one was called a Nocturn, now of late time a few of them have been daily said and the rest utterly omitted. .. So that here you have an Order for Prayer and for the Reading of the Holy Scripture much agreeable to the mind and purposes of the old fathers, and a great deal more profitable and commodious than that which of late was used.

This is conservatism in the very best sense, for the object aimed at is plainly the conservation of purity, simplicity, and truth, but surely it is not the conservatism of men with whom inaction is the only wisdom and immobility the sole beatitude.

We change our sky completely in passing from Anglo-Catholic to Broad Church criticism of *The Book Annexed*. This last has, in the main, addressed itself to

* See Wisconsin Report, p. 5.

the rubrical features of the proposed revision. "You promised us 'flexibility,'" the accusation runs, "but what you are really giving us is simply rigidity under a new form. Let things stay as they are, and we will undertake to find all the 'flexibility' we care to have, without help from legislation."

This criticism has at least the merit of intelligibility, for it directly antagonizes what was, without doubt, one main purpose with the revisers, namely, that of reviving respect for the rubrics by making compliance with their terms a more practicable thing.

Evidently what Broad Churchmen, or at least a section of them, would prefer is the prevalence of a general consent under which it shall be taken for granted that rubrics are not literally binding on the minister, but are to be stretched and adapted, at the discretion of the officiant, as the exigencies of times and seasons may suggest. It is urged that such a common understanding already in great measure exists; and that to enact new rubrics now, or to remodel old ones, would look like an attempt to revivify a principle of compliance which we have tacitly agreed to consider dead.

The answer to this argument is not far to seek. If the Church means to allow the Common Prayer, which hitherto has been regarded as a liturgy, to lapse into the *status* of a directory; if, in other words, she is content to see her manual of worship altered from a book of instructions as to how Divine Service *shall* be performed into a book of suggestions as to how it *may* be rendered, the change ought to be officially and definitely announced, and not left to individual inference or uncertain conjecture. We are rapidly slipping into a position scarcely consistent with either the dignity or the honor of a great Church—that of seeming to be what we are not. To give it out to the public that we are a law-respecting communion, and then to whisper it about among ourselves that our laws bind only those who choose to be bound by them, may serve as a convenient device for tiding over a present difficulty, but is, on the whole, a course of procedure more likely to harden than to relieve tender consciences.

Take, by way of illustration, the case of a city clergyman who would gladly introduce into his parish the usage of daily service, but who is convinced, whether rightly or wrongly, that to secure even a fair attendance of worshippers he ought to have the liberty of so far condensing the Morning or the Evening Office as to bring it within the limits of a quarter of an hour. He seeks relief through the lawful channel of rubrical revision, and is only laughed at for his pains. In this busy nineteenth century it is nonsense, he is assured, to spend a dozen years in besieging so obdurate a fortress as the General Convention. The way to secure "shortened services" is to shorten services. This is easy logic, and applicable in more directions than one. Only see how smoothly it runs: If you want hymns that are not in the Hymnal, print them. If you want a confessional-box, set it up. If you want a "reserved sacrament," order the carpenter to make a tabernacle and the locksmith to provide a bolt.* This is a far less troublesome method of securing the ends desired than the tedious and roundabout process of proposing a change at one

---

* See the precautions recommended in *The Living Church Annual* for 1886, p. 132, art "Tabernacle."

meeting of the General Convention, having your proposal knocked about among some forty or fifty dioceses, and brought up for final action three years later.

And yet, superior as the former method may be to the latter in point of celerity and directness, the latter has certain advantages over the former that ought to be evident to men who are not frightened by having their scrupulousness called scrupulosity.

Moreover, why should this whole matter be discussed, as so commonly it is discussed, wholly from the clerical side? Have the laity no rights in the liturgy which the clergy are bound to respect? When and where did the Protestant Episcopal Church confer on its ministers a general dispensing power over the ordinances of worship which it withheld from the body of the faithful?

Heretofore it has been held that when a layman went to church he had a right to expect certain things guaranteed him by the Church's law. If all this has been changed, then formal notice ought to be served upon us by the General Convention that such is the fact.

THE MOTIVE OF THE EFFORT AFTER REVISION.

It is asked, and with no little show of plausibility, Why—in the face of such manifold hostility and such persistent opposition, why press the movement for revision any further? Is it worth while to divide public sentiment in the Church upon a question that looks to many to be scarcely more than a literary one? Why not drop the whole thing, and let it fall into the limbo, where lie already the *Proposed Book* and the *Memorial Papers?* For this reason, and it is sufficient: There has arisen in America a movement toward Christian unity, the like of which has not been seen since the country was settled. It is the confident belief of many that the key to the situation lies with that Church which more truly than any other may be said to represent the historical Christianity of the peoples of English stock. One of the elements in this larger movement is the question of the form of worship. The chief significance of *The Book Annexed* lies in the claim made for it by its friends, that more adequately than the present Standard it supplies what may fairly be demanded as their manual of worship by a people circumstanced like ours. While, in one sense, more English than the present book in that it restores liturgical treasures lost at the Revolution, it is also more thoroughly American, in that it recognizes and allows for many needs which the newly enfranchised colonists of 1789 could not have been expected to foresee.

The question is, Shall we turn a cold shoulder on the movement churchward of our non-Anglican brethren of the reformed faith, doing our best to chill their approaches with a hard *Non possumus*, or shall we go out to meet them with words of welcome on our lips? Union under "the Latin obedience" is impossible. For us, in the face of the decrees of 1870, there can be "no peace with Rome." The Greeks are a good way off. Our true "solidarity," if "solidarity" is to be achieved at all, is not with Celts, but with our own kith and kin, the children of the Reformation. Is it wise of us to say to these fellow Christians of ours, adherents of the Catholic Faith as well as we, "Nay, but the nearer you draw to us the farther we mean to draw away from you; the more closely you approximate to Anglican religion, the more closely shall we, for the sake of differencing ourselves from you, approximate to Vatican religion?"

In better harmony with the apostolic temper, in truer continuity with the early churchmanship, should we be found, were we to join voices thus:

V. Come ye, and let us walk in the light of the Lord.

R. And he will teach us of his ways, and we will walk in his paths.

II.

THE *Book Annexed* may be said to hold to the possible standard Common Prayer of 1890 a relation not unlike that of a clay model to the statue which is to be. The material is still in condition to be moulded; the end is not yet. It was in anticipation of this state of things that the friends of revision in 1883 were anxious to carry through the preliminary stage of acceptance as many of their propositions as possible. To revert to our parable, the modeller, in treating the face of his provisional image, must be careful to lay on clay enough, or he may find himself barred at the last moment from giving the features just that finishing touch which is to make them ready for the marble. All the skill in the world will not enable him to secure for the face precisely the expression he would have it wear, if the *materia* be insufficient. Looked at in this light, the suggestion made by the Joint Committee in the House of Deputies at an early stage of the session of 1883, that the entire *Book Annexed*, in precisely the form in which it had been submitted, should be passed, and sent down to the dioceses for consideration, instead of being the arbitrary and unreasonable demand it was reckoned by those who lifted their eyebrows at the very mention of such a thing, was really a sensible proposition which the Convention would have done well to heed.

Few, if any, critics of *The Book Annexed as Modified* have pronounced it an improvement to *The Book*

Annexed as presented. The Book came out of the Convention less admirable than it went in. As a school of Liturgics, the long debate at Philadelphia was doubtless salutary and helpful, but whether the immediate results, as shown in the emendation of the Joint Committee's work, were equally deserving of praise is another question.

Nevertheless, as was argued in the paper of which this one is the continuation, we must take things as we find them, not as we wish they were; and since there is no other method of liturgical revision known to our laws than revision by popular debate, to revision by popular debate we must reconcile ourselves as best we may. Regrets are idle. Let us be thankful that the amicable struggle at Philadelphia had for its outcome so large rather than so small a mass of workable material, and instead of accounting *The Book Annexed* to be what one of the signers of the Joint Committee's Report has lately called it, "a melancholy production," recognize in it the germ of something exceedingly to be desired. From the first, there has never been any disposition on the part of sober-minded friends of Revision to carry through their scheme with a rush; the delay that is likely to better things they will welcome; the only delay they deprecate is the delay that kills.

The changes enumerated in the "Notification to the Dioceses," and illustrated to the eye in *The Book Annexed as Modified*, may be broadly classified under the following heads:

(*a*) Clearly desirable alterations, with respect to which there is practically unanimous consent, and for which there is immediate demand, *e. g.*, shortened offices of week-day prayer.

(*b*) Alterations desirable in the main, but likely to be more cordially acquiesced in, could still further improvement be secured, *e. g.*, the new versicles introduced into Evening Prayer after the Creed.

(*c*) Alterations generally accounted undesirable on any terms, *e. g.*, the permissive rubrics with respect to the reading of certain psalms during Lent, instead of the regular responds to the First and Second Lessons of the Evening Prayer.

The question arises, Is any course of action possible that will give us without delay the changes which for some fifteen years the whole Church has been laboring to secure ; that will give us, with a reasonable delay of three years longer, the confessed improvements a little more improved ; while at the same time we are kept from becoming involved in the wretched confusion sure to result from putting into circulation, within a brief period, two authorized but diverse books of Common Prayer? This threefold question it is proposed to meet with a threefold affirmative.

THE STANDARD PRAYER BOOK OF 1890.

The end we ought to have in view is the publication, in the year 1890, of a standard Book of Common Prayer, such as shall embody the ripe results of what will then have been a period of ten years of continuous labor in the work of liturgical revision. To this reckoning of ten years should properly be added the seventeen years that intervened between the presentation of "The Memorial" in 1853 and the passing of the "Enrichment Resolutions" in 1880 : so that really our Revision would look back for its historical beginnings, not across a decade merely, but over almost the lifetime of a generation. No single one of the various revisions of the English Book has observed anything like so leisurely a movement.

But by what methods of legislative procedure could such a result as the one indicated be reached? The precedent of the last century does not help us very much. The American Book of Common Prayer was set forth on the sixteenth day of October in the year of our Lord 1789; but with an express statutory provision that the "use" of the book, as so set forth, should not become obligatory till the first day of October, 1790. We cannot copy this line of procedure, for the simple reason that no such undertaking as that of 1789 is in hand. It is not now proposed to legislate into existence a new Liturgy. The task before us is the far humbler one of passing judgment upon certain propositions of change, almost every one of which admits of segregation, has an independent identity of its own, and may be accepted or rejected wholly without reference to what is likely to happen to the other propositions that accompany it.

The Book Annexed as Modified is in no proper sense a *Proposed Book*, nor can it without misrepresentation be called such; it is simply a sample publication* illustrative of what the Book of Common Prayer would be, were all the Resolutions of Revision

* In this respect *The Book Annexed* may be compared to *The Convocation Prayer Book* published by Murray in 1880, for the purpose of showing what the English Book would be like if "amended in conformity with the recommendations of the Convocations of Canterbury and York, contained in reports presented to her Majesty the Queen in the year 1879."

that passed their first stage of approval in 1883 carried into final effect; a result most unlikely to occur.

THE MEANS TO THE END.

The most expeditious and every way satisfactory means to the end that has now been defined would be the appointment, at an early stage of the session in October, of a Joint Committee of Conference. To this committee should be referred:

(*a*) The question: How many of the Resolutions of 1883, or of the "several recommendations therein contained," is it either practicable or desirable to approve at once?

(*b*) The question: How may such of the Resolutions of 1883 as are too good to be lost, but not in their present form good enough to satisfy the Church, be so remoulded as to make their adoption probable in 1889?

(*c*) All new propositions of improvement that may from time to time during the session be brought to the notice of the Convention, either by individual members or by memorials from Diocesan Conventions. Such a Committee of Conference, holding daily sessions of three or four hours each, would be able in due time to report a carefully digested scheme which could then be intelligently discussed. By this method a flood of frivolous and aimless talk would be cut off without in the slightest degree infringing or limiting the real liberty of debate.

But even if the Convention were to show itself reluctant to give to a select committee so large a power as this of preparing an *agenda* paper, it still would be possible to refer to such a committee the subject-matter of so many of the resolutions as might chance, when put upon their passage, to fail by a narrow vote.

It is to be remembered that the various recommendations contained in the resolutions of 1883 are to be voted upon *in ipsissimis verbis*. There will be no opportunity for the familiar cry : " Mr. President, I rise to propose an amendment." The resolution, or the section of a resolution, as the case may be, will either be approved just as it stands or condemned just as it stands. In this respect there will be an immense saving of time. Most of the tediousness of debate grows out of the natural disposition of legislators to try each his own hand at bettering the thing proposed ; hence "amendments," "amendments to amendments," and substitutes for the amendment to the amendment. Even the makers of parliamentary law (much enduring creatures) lose their patience at this point, and peremptorily lay it down that confusion shall no further go.

But to return to the supposed case of a proposition lost because of some slight defect, which, if only our Medo-Persian law had permitted an amendment, could easily have been remedied. Surely the sensible course in such a case as that would be to refer the subject-matter of the lost resolution to the Committee of Conference, with instructions to report a new resolution to be finally acted upon three years hence. So then, whether there be given to the Committee of Conference either the large power to recommend a carefully thought out way of dealing with all the material *en bloc*, or the lesser function of sitting in judgment on new propositions, and of remoulding rejected ones, in either case there could scarcely fail to result from the appointment of such a committee large and substantial gains.

IMPROVEMENTS.

It follows, from what has been said, that if there are features that admit of improvement in the proposals which the Convention has laid before the Church for scrutiny, now is emphatically the time for suggesting the better thing that might be done. Even the bitterest opponents of *The Book Annexed* can scarcely be so sanguine as to imagine that nothing at all is coming from this labored movement for revision. A measure which was so far forth acceptable to the accredited representatives of the Church, in council assembled, as to pass its first stage three years ago almost by acclamation, is not destined to experience total collapse. The law of probabilities forbids the supposition. The personal make-up of the next General Convention will be to a great extent identical with that of the last, and of the one before the last. Sober-minded men familiar with the work of legislation are not accustomed to reverse their own well considered decisions without weighty cause. The strong probability is that something in the line of emendation, precisely how much or how little no one can say, will, as a matter of fact, be done. In view of this likelihood, would not those who are dissatisfied with *The Book Annexed* as it stands be taking the wiser course were they to substitute co-operative for vituperative criticism? So far as the present writer is in any sense authorized to speak for the friends of revision, he can assure the dissidents that such co-operation would be most welcome.

A. B., a scholar thoroughly familiar, we will suppose,

with the sources of liturgical material, is dissatisfied with the collects proposed for the successive days of Holy Week. Very well, he has a perfect right to his dissatisfaction and to the expression of it in the strongest terms at his command. He does only his plain duty in seeking to exclude from the Prayer Book anything that seems to him unworthy of a place in it. But seeing that he must needs, as a "liturgical expert," acknowledge that the deficiency which the Joint Committee sought to make good is a real and not a merely fancied deficiency, would not A. B. approve himself a more judicious counsellor if, instead of bending all his energy to the disparagement of the collects proposed, he should devote a portion of it to the discovery and suggestion of prayers more happily worded?

And this remark holds good with reference to whatever new feature is to be found between the covers of *The Book Annexed.* If betterment be possible, these six months now lying before us afford the time of all times in which to show how, with the least of loss and most of gain, it may be brought about.

The Diocese of Maryland is first in the field with an adequate contribution of this sort. A thoroughly competent committee, appointed in October, 1884, has recently printed its Report, and whether the Diocesan Convention adopt, amend, or reject what is presented to it, there can be little doubt that the mind of the Church at large will be perceptibly affected by what these representative men of Maryland have said.* Apart from a certain aroma of omniscience pervading it (with which, by the way, sundry infelicities of language in the text

* The Report was adopted.

of the Report, only indifferently consort), the document is a forcible one, and of great practical value.

The Committee have gone over the entire field covered by the "Notification to the Dioceses," taking up the Resolutions one by one, and not only noting in connection with each whatever is in itself objectionable, but also (a far more difficult task) suggesting in what respect this or that proposition might be better put. The *apparatus criticus* thus provided, while not infallible, is eminently helpful, sets a wholesome pattern, and if supplemented by others of like tenor and scope, will go far to lighten the labor of whatever committee may have the final recension of the whole work put into its hands.*

It would be a poor self-conceit in the framers of *The Book Annexed*, that should prompt them to resent as intrusive any criticism whatsoever. What we all have at heart is the bringing of our manual of worship as nearly as possible to such a pitch of perfectness as the nature of things human will allow. The thing we seek is a Liturgy which shall draw to itself everything that is best and most devout within our national borders, a Common Prayer suited to the common wants of all Americans. Whatever truly makes for this end, it will be our wisdom to welcome, whether those who bring it forward are popularly labelled as belonging to this, that, or the other school of Churchmanship. To allow party jealousies to mar the symmetry and fulness of a work in which all Churchmen ought to have an equal inheritance would be the worst of blunders. By all

* In addition to the Maryland Report we have now a still more admirable one from Central New York.

means let the raiment of needlework and the clothing of wrought gold be what they should be for such sacred uses as hers who is the daughter of the great King, but let us not fall to wrangling about the vats in which the thread was dyed or the river bed from which the gold was gathered.

In a later paper the present writer intends to venture upon a task similar to that undertaken by the Maryland Committee. He will do this largely in the hope of encouraging by example other and more competent critics to busy themselves in the same way. Meanwhile a few observations may not be amiss with respect to the sources of liturgical material, and the methods by which they can be drawn upon to the best advantage.

There has been, first and last, a deal of ill considered talk about the boundlessness of the liturgical treasures lying unused in the pre-Reformation formularies of the English Church, as well as in the old sacramentaries and office-books of the East and the West. Wonder is expressed that with such limitless wealth at its command, an " Enrichment Committee " should have brought in so poverty-stricken a Report. Have we not Muratori and Mabillon? it is asked: Daniel and Assemani, Renaudot and Goar? Are there not Missals Roman, Ambrosian, and Mozarabic? Breviaries Anglican, Gallican, and Quignonian? Has Maskell delved and Neale translated and Littledale compiled in vain? To all of which there are two replies, namely: first, It is inexpedient to overload a Prayer Book, even if the material be of the best ; and secondly, This best material is by no means so abundant as the volume of our resources would seem to suggest. It was for the very purpose of escaping redundancy and getting rid of surplusage that the Anglican Reformers condensed Missal, Breviary, and Rituale into the one small and handy volume known as the First Prayer Book of Edward VI. It was a bold stroke, doubtless denounced as perilously radical at the time; but experience has justified Cranmer and his friends. In the whole history of liturgics there is no record of a wiser step. It is scarcely possible so grievously to sin against a people's Prayer Book as by making it more complicated in arrangement and more bulky in volume than need actually requires. It was ground of justifiable pride with the "Enrichment Committee" that the Book which they brought in, despite the many additions it contained, was no thicker by a single page than the Prayer Book as it is. To be sure, the General Convention spoiled all this by insisting on retaining certain duplicated formularies which the Committee had very properly dropped in order to find room for fresh material. But of the Book as first presented, it was possible to say that in no degree was it more cumbrous than that to which the people were already accustomed. Doubtless it would have been still more to the Committee's credit could they have brought in an enriched Book smaller by a third than the Book in use; but this their conservatism forbade.

Of even greater moment is the other point, which concerns the quality of the available material. It is the greatest mistake in the world to suppose that simply because a given prayer exists, say in an Oriental liturgy, and has been translated into English by an eminent scholar, it is therefore proper material to be worked into our services. As a matter of fact, a great deal of devotional language of which the Oriental liturgies is made up is prolix and tedious to a degree simply insufferable. Moreover in the case of prayers in themselves admirable in the original tongue in which they were composed, all is often lost through lack of a verbal felicity in the translation. If anyone questions this judgment, let him toil through Neale's and Littledale's *Translations of the Primitive Liturgies* and see whether he can find six, nay, three, consecutive lines which he would be willing to see introduced into our own Communion Office. Or, as respects translations from the Latin officebooks of the Church of England, let him scrupulously search the pages of the "Sarum Hours," as done into the vernacular by the Recorder of Salisbury, and see how many of the Collects strike him as good enough to be transplanted into the Book of Common Prayer. The result of this latter voyage of discovery will be an increased wonder at the affluence of the mediæval devotions, combined with amazement at the poverty and unsatisfactoriness of the existing translations. It is with a Latin collect as with a Greek ode or an Italian sonnet: no matter how wonderful the diction, the charm of it is as a locked secret until the thing has been Englished by genius akin to his who first made it out of his own heart. Of others besides the many brave men who lived before Agamemnon might it be written:

> sed omnes illacrumabiles
> Urgentur, ignotique larga
> Nocte, carent quia vate sacro

It was the peculiar felicity of Schiller that he had Coleridge for a translator, and the shades of Gregory and Leo owe it to a living Anglican divine that we English-speaking Christians can think their thoughts after them, and pray their prayers.

Such being the facts in the case, it is evident that the range of choice open to American revisers is far narrower than half-informed persons imagine it to be.

The very best sources of liturgical material are the following :

(*a*) King James's Bible, including the Apocrypha, and supplemented by the Prayer Book version of the Psalms ;

(*b*) The old Sacramentaries, Leonine, Gregorian, and Gelasian, chiefly as illustrated by the genius of Dr. Bright ;

(*c*) The Breviary in its various forms ;

(*d*) The Primers and other like *fragmenta* of the era of the English Reformation ; *

(*e*) The devotional writings of the great Anglican divines of the school of Andrews, Ken, and Taylor ; †
and last and least,

(*f*) The various manuals of prayer, of which the past twenty years have shown themselves so prolific. ‡

---

* Strangely enough the Elizabethan period, so rich in genius of every other type, seems to have been almost wholly barren of liturgical power. Men had not ceased to write prayers, as a stout volume in the Parker Society's Library abundantly evidences, but they had ceased to write them with the terseness and melody that give to the style of the great Churchmen of the earlier reigns so singular a charm.

† The liturgical manuscripts of Sanderson and Wren, made public only recently by the late Bishop of Chester, ought to be included under this head.

‡ Many of these "Treasuries," "Golden Gates," and the like, have

Of the Anglican writers, Jeremy Taylor would be by far the most helpful, were it not for the efflorescence of his style. As it is, the best use that can be made of his exuberant devotions is to cull from them here and there a telling phrase or a musical cadence. The "General Intercession," for example, on page 50 of *The Book Annexed*, is a cento to which Taylor is the chief contributor.

That the Enrichment Committee made the best possible use of the various quarries to which they had access is unlikely. Even if they credited themselves with having done so, it would be immodest of them to say it. Better material than any that their researches brought to light may still be lying near the surface, somewhere close at hand, waiting to be unearthed. Certainly this paper will not have been written in vain if it serves the purpose of provoking to the good work of discovery some of those who on the score both of quality and of quantity account what has been thus far done in the line of revision inadequate and meagre.

here and there something good, but for the most part they are disfigured by sins against that "sober standard of feeling," than which, as a high authority assures us, nothing except "a sound rule of faith" is more important "in matters of practical religion." Of all of them, Scudamore's unpretentious little "Manual" is, perhaps, the best.

III.

It is next proposed to take up the Philadelphia Resolutions of Revision (1883) one by one, and to consider in what measure, if in any, the subject-matter of each of them lies open to improvement.

Should the method of procedure recommended in the previous paper, or any method resembling it, find favor at the approaching Convention, and a Conference Committee of the two Houses be appointed to remould the work with reference to final action three years hence, criticism of this sort, even though inadequate, can scarcely fail of being in some measure helpful.

RESOLUTION I.

The Title-page.

The proposals under this head are two in number: (*a*) that the words, "together with the Psalter or Psalms of David," be dropped from the title-page as superfluous, and (*b*) that a general title, "THE BOOK OF COMMON PRAYER," be printed on the first page of the leaf preceding the title-page.

Neither of these suggestions is of any great importance, and the interest attaching to them is mainly bibliographical. Whenever any addition has been made to the Prayer Book of the Church of England, the rule has been to note it invariably in the Table of Contents, and sometimes also on the title-page.

Until 1662 the Psalter formed no part of the Prayer

Book; it was a volume by itself, and was cited as such. In fact, it was a sort of "Hymnal Companion to the Book of Common Prayer." In the revision of 1662 the Psalter was incorporated, and immediately there appeared upon the title-page of the Common Prayer, in addition to what had been there before, the words, "together with the Psalter or Psalms of David printed as they are to be sung or read in the churches." The present title-page of the English Book has a singularly crowded and awkward look, contrasting most unfavorably in this regard with those of 1559, 1552, and 1549.*
But if the needless mention of the Psalter on our present title-page gives pleasure to any considerable number of people, it would be foolish to press the suggestion of a change. Let it pass.

Of a more serious character would be the omission, which some urge, of the words "Protestant Episcopal" from the title-page. Should anything of this sort be done, which is most unlikely, Dr. Egar's suggestion to drop the words, "of the Protestant Episcopal Church," leaving it to read, "according to the use in the United States of America," would carry the better note of catholicity.

But, after all, the remonstrants have only to turn the page to find the obnoxious "Protestant Episcopal" so fast riveted into the *Ratification* that nothing short of an act of violence done to history could accomplish the excision of it. †

---

* For a *conspectus* of the various title-pages, see Keeling's *Litugiæ Britannicæ*, London, 1842.

† The question of a change in the name of the Church is a constitutional, and in no sense a liturgical question. Let it be considered at the proper time, and in a proper way, but why thrust it precipitately into a discussion to which it is thoroughly foreign ?

RESOLUTION II.

The Introductory Portion.

(a) *Table of Contents.*—The suggestion * that all entries after "The Psalter" should be printed in italics, is a good one.

(b) *Concerning the Service of the Church.*—This substitute for the present "Order how the Psalter is appointed to be read" and "Order how the rest of the Holy Scripture is appointed to be read" is largely based on the provisions of the so-called "Shortened Services Act" of 1872. The second paragraph relating to the use of the Litany appears to be superfluous.

The enlarged Table of Proper Psalms and the Table of Selections of Psalms, which come under this same general heading, would be a very great gain. Why the Maryland Committee should have pronounced the latter Table "practically useless, since the psalms are not to be printed," it is hard, in the face of the existing usage with respect to "Proper Psalms," to understand; nor is there any special felicity in the proposal emanating from the same source that the number of the Selections be cut down to three, one for feasts and one for fasts and one for an extra service on Sunday nights.

On the other hand, the Maryland Committee does well in recommending that permission be given to the minister to shorten the Lessons at his discretion, though the hard and fast condition, "provided he read not less than fifteen consecutive verses," apart from the ques-

---

* By the Maryland Committee.

tionable English in which it is phrased, smacks more of the drill-room than of the sanctuary. Far better would it be (if the suggestion may be ventured) to allow no liberty of abridgment whatever in the case of Proper Lessons, while giving entire freedom of choice on all occasions for which no proper lessons have been appointed. So far as "ferial" days are concerned, it would be much wiser to let the Table of Lessons be regarded as suggestive and not mandatory. The half-way recognition of this principle in the new Lectionary, in which such a freedom is allowed, *provided* the Lesson taken be one of those appointed for "some day in the same week," seems open to a suspicion of childishness.

The rubrical direction entitled "Hymns and Anthems" requires verbal correction, but embodies a wholesome principle.

Under this same general head of "The Introductory Portion" come the new Lectionary and the new Tables for finding Easter. Of these, the former is law already, except so far as respects the Lessons appointed for the proposed Feast of the Transfiguration. The Easter Tables are a monument to the erudition and accuracy of the late Dr. Francis Harison. The Tables in our present Standard run to the year 1899. Perhaps a "wholesome conservatism" ought to discover a tincture of impiety in any proposal to disturb them before the century has expired.

RESOLUTION III.

The Morning Prayer.

(a) *The First Rubric.*—The Maryland Committee is quite right in remarking that the language of this important rubric, as set forth by the Convention of 1883, is "inelegant and inaccurate," but another diocese has called attention to the fact that the substitute which Maryland offers would, if adopted, enable any rector who might be so minded to withhold entirely from the non-communicating portion of his flock all opportunity for *public* confession and absolution from year's end to year's end. It is not for a moment to be supposed that there was any covert intention here, but the incident illustrates the value to rubric-makers of the Horatian warning—*Brevis esse laboro, obscurus fio.*

Passing by the Proper Sentences for special Days and Seasons, against which no serious complaint has been entered,* we come to the proposed short alternative for the Declaration of Absolution. As it stood in the Sarum Use this Absolution ran as follows:

"The Almighty and Merciful Lord grant you Absolution and Remission of all your sins, space for true penitence, amendment of life, and the grace and consolation of the Holy Spirit. Amen." †

With the single change of the word "penitence" to

---

* This paragraph was written before the author had been privileged to read Prof. Gold's interesting paper in *The Seminarian*. It is only proper to say that this accomplished writer and very competent critic does object emphatically to the theory that the opening Sentences are designed to give the key-note of the Service. But here he differs with Blunt, as elsewhere in the same paper he dissents from Freeman and from Littledale, admirably illustrating by his proper assertion of an independent judgment, the difficulty of applying the Vicentian rule in liturgical criticism. Such variations of opinion do, indeed, make against "science," but they favor good sense.

† Chambers's Translation.

"repentance" this is the form in which the Absolution stood in the original *Book Annexed*. The Convention thought that it detected a "Romanizing germ" in the place assigned to "penitence," and an archaism in the temporal sense assigned to "space," and accordingly rearranged the whole sentence. But in their effort to mend the language, our legislators assuredly marred the music.*

(e) *The Benedictus es, Domine.*—The insertion of this Canticle as an alternate to the *Te Deum* was in the interest of shortened services for week-day use, as has been already explained. The same purpose could be served equally well, and the always objectionable expedient of a second alternate avoided, by spacing off the last six verses of the *Benedicite*, which have an integrity of their own, and prefixing a rubric similar to those that stand before the *Venite* and the *Benedictus* in "The Book Annexed"; *e. g.:*

¶ *On week-days, it shall suffice if only the latter portion of this Canticle be said or sung.*

(n) *The Benedictus.*—With reference to the restoration of the last portion of this Hymn, it has been very properly remarked by one of the critics of *The Book Annexed*, that the line of division between the required and the optional portions would more properly come after the eighth than after the fourth verse. This

---

* This is not to be understood as an acknowledgment that the doctrinal and philological objections to the formulary as it originally stood were sound and sufficient. On the lips of a Church which declares "repentance" to be an act whereby we "forsake sin," a prayer for time does not seem wholly inappropriate, while as for this use of the word "space" of which complaint was made, it should be noticed that King James's Bible gives us nineteen precedents for it; and the Prayer Book itself one.

would make the portion reserved for Advent begin with the reference to John the Baptist, as undoubtedly it ought to do: "And thou, child, shalt be called the Prophet of the Highest."

(o) *De Profundis.*—There will probably be general consent to the omission of this alternate, as being what the Maryland Committee *naïvely* call it, "too mournful a psalm" for this purpose.*

RESOLUTION IV.

Daily Evening Prayer.

(c) The proposed words, "Let us humbly confess our sins unto Almighty God," are justly thought by many to be inferior both in rhythm and in dignity to "Let us make humble confession to Almighty God."

(i)-(l) There seems to be absolute unanimity in the judgment that *Magnificat* and *Nunc Dimittis* ought, as Gospel Hymns, to have the prior places after the Lessons which they follow. In the interest of sim-

---

* In *The Book Annexed*, as originally presented, there stood in this place the beautiful and appropriate psalm, *Levavi oculos*. But the experts declared that this would never do, since from time immemorial *Levavi oculos* had been a Vesper Psalm, and it would be little less than sacrilege to insert it in a morning service, however congruous to such a use the wording of it might, to an unscientific mind, appear. Accordingly the excision was made; but upon inquiry it turned out that the monks had possessed a larger measure of good sense, as well as a better exegesis, than the Convention had attributed to them, for *Levavi oculos*, it appears, besides being a Vesper psalm, stood assigned, in the Sarum Breviary, to Prime as well, the fact being that the psalm is alike adapted to morning and to evening use, and singularly appropriate both to the "going out" and the "coming in" of the daily life of man.

plicity of arrangement a like general consent to omit altogether *Bonum est confiteri* and *Benedic anima mea* would be most fortunate, but this point has been already enlarged upon in a previous paper.*

The "¶ Notes," permitting the use of Psalms xlii. and xliii. after the Lessons during Lent, seem to have found no favor in any quarter, and ought undoubtedly to be dropped.

(n) If the lost versicles are to be restored after the Creed, as all who have learned to love them in the service of the Church of England must earnestly desire, some better substitute for "God save the queen," than "O Lord, save our rulers," ought surely to be found.† Moreover, the order of the versicles, as Prof. Gold has clearly pointed out,‡ is open to improvement.

RESOLUTION V.

The Beatitudes of the Gospel.

This is the one feature of *The Book Annexed* against which the fire of hostile criticism has been the most persistently directed. Whether the strictures passed upon the Office have been in all cases as intelligent as

* See p. 6.

† "O Lord, bow thine ear," has been suggested as a substitute. It is in the words of Holy Scripture, it is the precise metrical equivalent of "O Lord, save the queen," and it is directly antiphonal to the versicle which follows.

There being no Established 'Church in the United States, it is doubtful whether any prayers for "rulers" are desirable, over and above those we already have. And if this point be conceded, the other considerations mentioned may be allowed to have weight in favor of "O Lord, bow thine ear."

‡ *The Seminarian*, 1886, pp. 29, 30.

they have been severe, may be open to question, but there can be no doubt whatever that, in its present form, RESOLUTION V. would, if put to the vote, be rejected.

Passing by the more violent utterances of those whose language almost suggests that they find something objectionable in the very BEATITUDES themselves,* it will suffice to consider and weigh what has been said in various quarters, first, about the unprecedented character of the Office, and secondly, concerning the infelicity of the appointed response, "Lord, have mercy upon us, and be it unto thy servants according to thy word."

So far as concerns precedent, it ought to be enough to say that the words are our Lord's words, and that they were thrown by him into a form which readily lends itself to antiphonal use. The very same characteristics of parallelism and antithesis, that make the Psalms so amenable to the purposes of worship, are conspicuous in the BEATITUDES. If the Church of England, for

* It may be well to throw into a foot-note a single illustration of what might otherwise be thought an extravagant statement. The Rev. W. C. Bishop, writing in *The Church Eclectic* for February, 1884, says:

"The service of the Beatitudes proposed by the Committee is just one of 'fancy-liturgy making,' which ought to be summarily rejected. We have more than enough of this sort of thing already; the commandments, comfortable words, *et hoc genus omne*, are anything but 'unique glories' of our Liturgy. Anything of which we have exclusive possession is nearly certain to be a 'unique *blunder*,' instead of anything better, because the chances are a thousand to one that anything really beautiful or edifying would have been discovered by, and have commended itself to, some other Christians in the last two thousand years." If such is to be the nomenclature of our new "science," Devotion may well stand aghast in the face of Liturgics.

three hundred years, has been willing to give place in her devotions to the Curses of the Old Testament,* we of America need not to be afraid, precedent or no precedent, to make room among our formularies for the Blessings of the New.

Those who allow themselves to characterize the liturgical use of these memorable sayings of the Son of Man as "fancy ritual" and "sentimentalism" may well pause to ask themselves what manner of spirit they are of. The BEATITUDES are the charter of the kingdom of heaven. If they are "sentimental," the kingdom is "sentimental"; but if, on the other hand, they constitute the organic law of the People of God, they have at least as fair a right as the Ten Commandments to be published from the altar, and answered by the great congregation.

But is the complaint of "no precedent" a valid one, even supposing considerations of intrinsic fitness to have been ruled out?

The Liturgy of St. Chrysostom provides that the Beatitudes shall be sung on Sundays in room of the third antiphon.†

The learned Bishop of Haiti, in a paper warmly commending the liturgical use of the BEATITUDES,‡ calls attention to the further fact that the Eight Sayings

* See the Commination Office in the Prayer Book of the Church of England

† Daniel's *Codex Liturgicus*, vol iv p. 343. Quoted in *Dictionary of Christian Antiquities* The translation of μακαρισμοί has been doubted, but Dr Neale and Prof Cheetham agree that the reference is to the BEATITUDES of the Gospel.

‡ *Church Eclectic* for April, 1884

have a place in some of the service-books of the Eastern Church in the Office for the Sixth and Ninth Hours, and notes the suggestive and touching circumstances that, as there used, they have for a response the words of the penitent thief upon the cross. We might all of us well pray to be "remembered" in that kingdom to which these Blessings give the law.

In *The Primer set forth by the King's Majesty and his Clergy* in 1545, a sort of stepping-stone to the later "Book of Common Prayer," we find the BEATITUDES very ingeniously worked into the Office of The Hours, as anthems; beginning with Prime and ending with Evensong. Appropriate Collects are interwoven, some of them so beautiful as to be well worth preserving.*

But the most interesting precedent of all remains still to be studied. In the first year of the reign of William and Mary, a Royal Commission was appointed to revise the Book of Common Prayer. The most eminent Angli-

---

* The following will serve as an illustration
The Anthem:
Blessed are the merciful, for they shall get mercy; blessed are the clean in the heart, for they shall see God.
The Versicle:
Lord hear my prayer.
The Answer:
And let my cry come to thee.
Let us pray.
Lord Jesu Christ, whose property is to be merciful, which art alway pure and clean without spot of sin; Grant us the grace to follow thee in mercifulness toward our neighbors, and always to bear a pure heart and a clean conscience toward thee, that we may after this life see thee in thy everlasting glory, which livest and reignest God, world without end *Amen.*

can divines of the day, including Tillotson, Stillingfleet, Patrick, and Beveridge, were among the members. To all outward appearance the movement came to naught; for the proposed revision was not even put into print, until in 1854, the House of Commons, in response to a motion of Mr. Heywood, ordered it to be published as a Blue-book. And yet in some way our American revisers of 1789 must have found access to the original volume as it lay hidden in the archbishop's library at Lambeth; for not only does their work show probable evidence of such consultation, but in their Preface they distinctly refer to the effort of King William's Commission as a "great and good work,"* a thing they would scarcely have done had they possessed no real knowledge of the facts. Macaulay's sneering reference to the work of the Commission is well known, but, strangely enough, the justice which a Whig reviewer withholds, a high Anglican divine concedes, for no less exacting a critic than Dr. Neale, while manifesting, as was to be expected, a general dislike of the Commissioners of 1689, and of their work, does yet find something to praise in what they recommended.†

Among the real improvements suggested by the Commission was the liturgical use of the BEATITUDES, and this in two places, once in "The Order for the Administration of the Lord's Supper," as an alternate to the Ten Commandments; and again in the Commination

---

* It is interesting and suggestive to observe with how much less frequency our attention is called to this paragraph of the Preface than to the later one which asserts historical continuity with the Church of England.

† *Essays on Liturgiology*, p. 226.

Office as a proper balance to the Anathemas of the Law.

But the Commission, like the late Joint Committee on the Book of Common Prayer, was unfortunate in its choice of a response; and no wonder, for the task of finding the proper one is difficult.*

A Beatitude differs from a Commandment in that while the latter enjoins the former only declares. The one therefore simply calls for assent, or, at most, assent coupled with petition, while the other peremptorily demands a cry for mercy. The immemorial form of the cry for mercy in the devotions of Christendom is the "Kyrie eleison," *Lord, have mercy upon us;* the immemorial form of assent the word *Amen.* Can we do better, therefore, in adapting the BEATITUDES to liturgical use than to treat them precisely as the Curses are treated in the Commination Office of the Church of England, namely, by inserting after each one of them a plain *Amen?*

This recommendation has the great merit of simplicity. Two or three strikingly ingenious schemes for supplying each of the Eight Sayings with a proper response of its own have been suggested; † but the objection to them is that, beautiful though they are, their complexity would embarrass and distress the kneeling worshipper. In these matters, practical drawbacks have to be taken into account as well as abstract excellencies, and no

---

* The response proposed by the Commissioners ran, " Lord have mercy upon us, and make us partakers of this blessing," a prayer unobjectionable for substance, but painfully pedestrian in style.

† Notably one in which the responses are all taken from Psalm li.

matter how felicitous the antiphonal responses, they would be worse than useless were a puzzled congregation to refuse to join in them.

There will be found appended to this Paper a plan for recasting the Office of the BEATITUDES in such a way as to make it coincide structurally, as far as it goes, with the introductory portion of the Holy Communion.* Were the Office to be thus set forth, it would be possible on week-days, and with singular appropriateness on Saints' Days, to substitute the BEATITUDES for the COMMANDMENTS, without encumbering the Communion Office with an alternate. Should this suggestion find acceptance, the two Collects in the present Office of BEATITUDES, which are far too good to be lost, one of them being the modified form of a Leonine original, and the other one of the very best of Canon Bright's own compositions, might be transferred to a place among the "Occasional Prayers."

RESOLUTION VI.

The Litany.

The rubrics prefixed to the Litany are a gain, but except by the addition of the two new suffrages, the one for the President and the other for the increase of the ministry, it will probably be best to leave the text of this formulary untouched. Even in the case of the new petitions it would be well if they could be grafted upon suffrages already existing, a thing that might easily be done.†

* See Note at the end of this Paper.
† *E. g.:* " That it may please thee to send forth laborers into thy harvest, and to have mercy upon all men."

It would be a liturgical improvement if the Litany, in its shortened form, were to end at the *Christe, audi,* and the minister directed to return, at this point, to the General Thanksgiving in the Morning Prayer. This would divide the Litany symmetrically, instead of arbitrarily, as is now done, and would remove the General Thanksgiving from a place to which it has little claim either by historical precedent or natural congruity.

The greatest improvement of all would be the restoration of the august and massive words of invocation which of old stood at the beginning of the Litany. The modern invocations have a dignity of their own, but they are not to be compared for devotional power and simple majesty with the more ancient ones. But for an "enrichment" so good as this, it is too much to hope.

RESOLUTION VII.

Prayers and Thanksgivings.

The Maryland Committee * have much to say in criticism of this section, and offer many valuable suggestions, the best of them being a recommendation to print the Prayer entitled, "For Grace to speak the Truth in Love," in Canon Bright's own words. Some of their comments, on the other hand, suggest canons of criticism which, if applied to "The Prayer Book as it is," would make havoc of its choicest treasures.†

---

* See Report, pp. 6–9.

† "Strike it out," said the literalist of a certain committee on hymnody, many years ago, as he and his colleagues were sitting in judgment on Watts's noble hymn, "There is a land of pure

The Committee of Central New York* go much further in the line of destructive criticism than their brethren of Maryland, and after excepting four of the proposed prayers, condemn all the rest to dismissal.

Possibly this is just judgment, but those who have searched diligently the storehouses of devotional English, will think twice before they consent to it. No doubt the phraseology of some of the proposed prayers might be improved. In view of the searching criticism to which for three years it has been exposed, it would be strange indeed if such were not found to be the case. But the collection as a whole, instead of suffering loss, ought to receive increment. At least three or four more prayers for the work of missions in its various aspects ought to be added, also a Prayer for the furtherance of Christian Education in Schools and Colleges. As Dr. Dowden shrewdly asks, in speaking of spiritual needs which we postpone expressing for lack of language

delight." "Either strike out the whole hymn or alter that word, 'living.'

"'Bright fields, beyond the swelling flood,
Stand dressed in *living* green.'

What sense is there in 'living' green ? It is the grass that lives, not the green." Happily the suggestion failed to find a seconder. But revisers, whose work is to be passed upon by ballot, may well be shy of idiomatic English. Take such a phrase as, "Now for the comfortless trouble's sake of the needy", Lindley Murray, were he consulted, would have no mercy on it and yet a more beautiful and touching combination of words is not to be found anywhere in the Psalter. It is the utter lack of this idiomatic characteristic that makes "Lambeth prayers" proverbially so insipid.

*See Report, p 12.

sufficiently artistic in form, "What is the measure of our faith in the efficacy of united prayer, when we are content to go on, year after year, and never come together to ask God to supply those needs?"*

There is one consideration connected with this supply of special prayers too frequently lost out of sight. While it is perfectly true that the Book of Common Prayer was never designed to be a *Treasury of Devotion* for individuals, it is equally true that for thousands and hundreds of thousands of our fellow-countrymen who live remote from "Church book-stores," or lack the means of patronizing them, the Prayer Book is, as a matter of fact, their only devotional help. In countless households, moreover, many of them beyond "Protestant Episcopal" borders altogether, the Prayer Book is doing a work only less beneficent than it might do, were we to concede a very little more to that outwardly illogical but spiritually self-consistent policy which, breaking away, a century ago, from the chain of precedent, inserted in the American Book "The Forms of Prayer to be used in Families."

RESOLUTION VIII.

Penitential Office for Ash-Wednesday.

This is the English Commination Office, with the introductory portion omitted. It would add to the merit of the formulary, especially when used as a separate office, were it to be prefaced by the versicle and response, similarly employed in the Hereford Breviary:

* Quoted in *The Church Eclectic* for August, 1886.

V. Let us confess unto the Lord, for he is gracious.

R. And his mercy endureth forever.

In view of the great length of the Morning Service on Ash-Wednesday, and the close similarity between the closing portion of the Litany and the intermediate portion of this Office, the following emendation of the first Rubric is suggested, a change which would carry with it the omission of the Rubric after psalm li. a little further on.

¶ *On the* First *Day of Lent, at* Morning Prayer, *the Office ensuing shall be read immediately after the words,* Have mercy upon us, *in the Litany, and in place of what there followeth.*

In the third Rubric it might be well to add to "*shall be said*" the words, "*or sung.*"

The blessing at the end of the office should stand, as in the English Book, in the precatory form; otherwise we might have the anomaly of a benediction pronounced before the end of the service.

RESOLUTION IX.

Thanksgiving-day or Harvest-home.

The only alteration needed in this office is the restoration of the beautiful prayer for unity to its own proper wording as given in the so-called "Accession Service" appended to the English Prayer Book. As it stands in *The Book Annexed* the language of the prayer is possibly ungrammatical and certainly redundant. A critic, already more than once quoted,[*] protests against the prominence given to this office in *The Book An-*

---

[*] Prof. Gold in *The Seminarian,* p. 34.

nexed, ascribing it to influences born of the associations of New England. But although the motive of the revisers might have had a worse origin than that of which the reviewer complains, the actual fact is that the formulary was placed where it is purely in consideration of the liturgical fitness of things; it having been held that the proper position for an Office of Thanksgiving must be in immediate sequence to an Office of Penitence.

It is with sincere diffidence that the present writer differs with *The Seminarian*, on a point of historical precedent, but he ventures to suggest that to find the prototype of Harvest-home we must go back far beyond New England, and for that matter far beyond Old England, nay, beyond the Christian era itself, even to the day when it was said, "Thou shalt observe the Feast of Tabernacles, seven days, after that thou hast gathered in thy corn and thy wine." Doubtless there is a joy greater than the "joy of harvest," and to this we give expression in the Eucharist; but doubtless also the joy of harvest is in itself a proper joy and one which finds fitting utterance in such forms of prayer and praise as this.

RESOLUTION XI.

Collects, Epistles, and Gospels.

No department of liturgical revision calls for a nicer touch than that which includes the Collects. That new collects for certain unsupplied feasts and fasts would be a genuine enrichment of The Book of Common Prayer, has long been generally acknowledged among Anglican scholars. The most weighty fault to be found with the collects added by the revisers is that in too large proportion they are addressed to the second and third Persons of the Holy Trinity. The Eucharist itself, as a whole, is properly conceived of as addressed to the Eternal Father. The Collects, as forming part of the Eucharistic Office, ought, strictly speaking, to be also so addressed. It is true that there are exceptions to this rule, and they are found, some of them, in the Prayer Book as it is. But the revisers ought not to have altered the proportion so markedly as they have done, for whereas in our present Book the collects addressed to the Father are as eighty-three to three compared with those not so addressed, the ratio in *The Book Annexed* is that of eleven to three.

Moreover, there would seem to be no good reason for reverting to the usage of the First Book of Edward VI., which provides a second Collect, Epistle, and Gospel for the two great feasts of Christmas and Easter. A better way would be to take these additional collects, which are among the most beautiful in the language, and assign them respectively to the Sunday after Christmas, and the Monday in Easter-week.

RESOLUTION XII.

The Holy Communion.

To the few changes proposed in this Office, comparatively slight exception has been taken in any quarter. It will probably be wise to leave the language of the Prayer of Consecration wholly untouched, notwithstanding the alleged grammatical error near the end of it.

The Rubric which it has been proposed to append to the Office, touching the number of communicants without which it shall not be lawful to administer the Sacrament, being of a disciplinary rather than of a liturgical character, ought not to be urged. The proposal to transfer the Prayer of Humble Access to a place immediately before the Communion appears to be very generally acceptable.

It would relieve many worshippers who scruple as Christians at responding to the Fourth Commandment on the score of its Judaic character, if the language of the rubric prefixed to the Decalogue could contain, as did the corresponding rubric in Laud's Book for Scotland, a clause indicative of the mystical and spiritual sense in which the Law should be interpreted by those who live under the Gospel. But such a proposal would probably be accounted " of doctrine," and so be self-condemned.

Of the desirability of allowing a week-day use of the BEATITUDES in the room of the COMMANDMENTS enough has been already said.

RESOLUTION XVI.

Confirmation.

The permission to use a form of presentation instead of, or in addition to, the Preface is likely to be widely welcomed. The other *addenda* to this office, being apparently distasteful (for unlike reasons) to all the " schools of thoughts " in the Church, are likely to fail of acceptance ; and on the whole may easily be spared.

RESOLUTION XVIII.

Visitation of the Sick.

The proposed Commendatory Prayer, though in some of its features strikingly felicitous, is open to formal improvement. The addition of a short *Litany of the Dying* would be appreciated by those whose ministry is largely exercised among the sick.

RESOLUTION XX.

Burial of the Dead.

By far the most important section of this Resolution is the one providing for the insertion of special features when the office is used at the burial of children. The provision, or at least the suggestion, of a more appropriate Lesson would be wise, but for the rest, the office is almost all that could be wished.

A recent critic * raises the question, " Why single out infants alone for a special service? Why not forms for rich men and poor men—old men and maidens—widows and orphans ? " And yet our Lord Jesus Christ did single out little children in a very striking and wonderful manner, and drew a distinction between them and us which may well justify our treating their obsequies with a peculiar tenderness. Even Rome, *Mater dura infantum* as she has been sometimes thought, is studious to consult in this point the natural affections of the bereaved, and appoints a funeral mass distinct from that appointed for the dead in general.

Bishop Seabury felt the need of a rite of this sort and prepared one, but whether it was ever in actual use

* The Rev. Dr Robert in *The Churchman* for July 17, 1886.

among the clergy of Connecticut the writer is not informed. Many, very many, since Seabury's day, have felt the same need, and it is safe to say that no one feature of *The Book Annexed* has enjoyed so universal a welcome as this rightful concession to the demands of the parental heart.

CONCLUSION.

The survey of *corrigenda* is now complete. The list looks like a long one, but really the points noted are few compared with those which have passed unchallenged. Here and there in the Resolutions that have not been considered are words or phrases that admit of improvement, and which in an actual and authorized re-review by a Committee of Conference would undoubtedly be improved.

The bulk of the work has, for a period of three years, stood the incessant fire of a not always friendly criticism far better than could have been anticipated by those who in the first instance gave it shape. The difficulties of the task have been immense. That they have not all of them been successfully overcome is clear enough, but that they were faced with an honest purpose to be just and fair, and that this purpose was clung to persistently throughout, is a credit which Churchmen of the next generation will not withhold from those who sought to be of service to them.

It remains to be seen whether the representatives of the Church will take up this work and perfect it; or *per contra* in response to the demand for a "Commission of Experts," or the specious but utterly impracticable* proposal of concerted action with the Church of England, will decide to postpone the whole affair to the Greek Kalends. One thing is certain, to wit, that the death of this movement will mean inaction for at least a quarter of a century. The men do not live who will have the courage to embark on a fresh enterprise of the like purport while the shipwreck of this one is before their eyes. There are many who, out of a conscientious fear of disturbing what they like to think of as permanently settled, would view such a conclusion of the whole matter with profound gratitude to God. But there are many more to whom such a confession of the Church's inability to appreciate and unwillingness to meet the spiritual needs of a civilization wonderfully unlike anything that has preceded it would be most disheartening. Least of all is there valid ground for hope in the case of those who fancy that if they can only annihilate this project, the day will speedily come when they can revise the Prayer Book in a manner perfectly conformable to their own conception of the "Ideal Liturgy," and after a fashion which the most ardent Anglo-Catholic must fain approve.

The American Book of Common Prayer bears the impress to-day of two controlling minds, the mind of Seabury and the mind of White. Doubtless it stood written in the councils of the Divine Providence that so it should be. The two men represented respectively the two modes of apprehending spiritual truth which

---

* Specious, because our continuity with the Church life of England is inestimably precious; impracticable, because there is no representative body of the English Church authorized to treat with us.

have always been allowed counterplay and interaction in the history of English religion, and which always will be allowed such counterplay and interaction while English religion remains the comprehensive thing it is. No scheme of liturgical revision, no matter how scientifically constructed, will ever find acceptance with the people of this Church which does not do even-handed justice to both of the great historic growths which find their common root in Anglican soil.

When the spirit of Seabury shall have completely exorcised the spirit of White, or the spirit of White shall have completely exorcised the spirit of Seabury from the Church and from the Prayer Book, logic will have triumphed, as sixteen years ago it triumphed under the dome of St. Peter's—logical consistency will have triumphed, but catholicity will have fled.

NOTE.

THE BEATITUDES OF THE GOSPEL.

¶ *On* Christmas-day, Easter-day, *and* Whitsunday, *and on any week-day save* Ash-Wednesday *and* Good Friday, *this Office may be used in lieu of so much of* The Order for the Administration of the Lord's Supper *as precedeth the Epistle for the Day.*

¶ *This Office may also be used separately on occasions for which no proper Order hath been provided.*

¶ *The Minister standing up shall say the Lord's Prayer and the Collect following, the People kneeling, but the Lord's Prayer may be omitted if it hath been said immediately before.*

OUR Father, who art in heaven, Hallowed be thy Name. Thy kingdom come. Thy will be done on earth, As it is in heaven Give us this day our daily bread. And forgive us our trespasses, As we forgive those who trespass against us. And lead us not into temptation; But deliver us from evil. *Amen.*

The Collect.

ALMIGHTY God, unto whom all hearts are open, all desires known, and from whom no secrets are hid; Cleanse the thoughts of our hearts by the inspiration of thy Holy Spirit, that we may perfectly love thee, and worthily magnify thy holy Name; through Christ our Lord. *Amen.*

¶ *Then shall the Minister, turning to the People, rehearse the Eight Sayings of our Lord commonly called* THE BEATITUDES; *and the People, still kneeling, shall after every one of them reverently say* Amen.

Minister.

Jesus went up into a mountain; and his disciples came unto him. And he opened his mouth and taught them, saying: Blessed are the poor in spirit; for theirs is the kingdom of heaven.

Answer. Amen.

Minister. Blessed are they that mourn; for they shall be comforted.

Answer. Amen.

Minister. Blessed are the meek; for they shall inherit the earth.

Answer. Amen.

Minister Blessed are they which do hunger and thirst after righteousness; for they shall be filled.

Answer Amen.

Minister. Blessed are the pure in heart; for they shall see God.

Answer. Amen.

Minister. Blessed are the peace-makers; for they shall be called the children of God.

Answer. Amen.

Minister. Blessed are they which are persecuted for righteousness' sake; for theirs is the kingdom of heaven.

Answer. Amen.

Minister.

Hear also what the voice from heaven saith. Blessed are the dead who die in the Lord.

Answer.

Even so, saith the Spirit, for they rest from their labours.

Minister

Let us pray.

Almighty and Eternal God, to whom is never any prayer made without hope of mercy; Bow thine ear, we beseech thee, to our supplications, and in the country of peace and rest cause us to be made partners with thy holy servants; through Jesus Christ our Lord. Amen.*

¶ *Then shall be said the Collect for the Day and, unless the Holy Communion is immediately to follow, such other prayer or prayers, taken out of this Book, as the Minister shall think proper.*

* This Prayer has been gathered from the *Dirige* in *The Primer set forth by the King's Majesty and his Clergy*, 1545; the same source (it is interesting to note) to which we trace the English form of the *Collect for Purity* at the beginning of the office.

APPENDIX :

SERMONS BEFORE AND AFTER.

APPENDIX.

PERMANENT AND VARIABLE CHARACTERISTICS OF THE PRAYER BOOK.

A SERMON PREACHED IN ST. STEPHEN'S CHURCH, PHILADELPHIA, ON THE ANNIVERSARY OF THE BISHOP WHITE PRAYER BOOK SOCIETY, SUNDAY, NOVEMBER 24, 1878

One generation passeth away, and another generation cometh.—Eccles. i. 4.

AGAINST the background of this sombre fact of change, whatever there is in life that is stable stands out with a sharpness that compels notice. Just because the world is so full of variableness, our hearts' affections fasten with the tighter grip upon anything that seems to have the guarantees of permanence. The Book of Common Prayer appeals to us on this score, precisely as the Bible, in its larger measure, does · it is the book of many generations, not of one, and there is "the hiding of its power." We have received the Prayer Book from the generations that are gone, we purpose handing it on when "another generation cometh"; we hold it for the use and blessing of the generation which now is.

Our thoughts about the book, therefore, if we would have the thinking rightly done, must take hold upon the past, the present, and the future, a breadth of topic covered well enough perhaps by this phrase, The Permanent and the Variable Characteristics of the Prayer Book.

I make no apology for asking you to take up the subject in so grave a temper. Now, for more than three hundred years, the Common Prayer has been the manual of worship in use with the greater number of the people of that race which, meanwhile, in the providence of God, has been growing up to be the leading power on earth. Everywhere the English language seems to be going forth conquering and to conquer, and whithersoever it penetrates it carries with it the letters and the social traditions of a people whose character has been largely moulded by the influences of the Prayer Book. Africans, Indians, Hindoos are to-day, even in their heathenism, feeling the effects of waves of movement which throb from this centre. Men in authority, the world over, are living out, with more or less of consistency and thoroughness, those convictions about our duty toward God, and our duty toward our neighbor, which were early inwrought into their consciences through the instrumentality of these venerable forms. Surely no one can afford to think or speak otherwise than most seriously and carefully with regard to a book which has behind it a history so worthy, so rich, so pregnant with promise for the future.

Look first, then, at the power which the Prayer Book draws from its affiliations with the past. It is a common remark, so common as to be commonplace, that our liturgy owes its excellence to the fact of its not having been the composition or compilation of any one man. So much is evident enough upon the face of it: for a form of worship devised off-hand by an individual, or even put together by a committee sitting around a table, could scarcely be wholly satisfactory to any save the maker or the makers of it. But it is more to the purpose to observe that not only is the Prayer Book not the result of any one man's or any one committee's labors; it is not the work even of any one generation, or of any one age.

The men who gradually put the Prayer Book into what is substantially its present shape, in the days of Edward VI. and of Elizabeth, were no more the makers of the Prayer Book than were the men who, in a later reign, set forth what we call " the authorized version " of the Holy Scriptures, the first translators of the Bible. In both cases the work done was a work of review and revision. A much more severe review, a vastly more sweeping revision in the case of the Prayer Book than in the case of the Bible, I grant, but still, mainly a work of review and revision after all. "Continuity," that characteristic so precious in the eye of modern science, continuity marked the whole process.

The first Prayer Book of the Reformed Church of England was a condensed, simplified, and purified combination of formularies of worship already in use in the National Church. A certain amount of new material, some of it home made, some of it drawn from foreign sources, was added, but the great bulk of the new service-book had been contained in one or other of the older manuals. The Reformers did but clip and prune, with that exquisite taste and judgment which belong by tradition to English gardeners, the overgrowth and rank luxuriance of a too long neglected, "careless-ordered" garden But whence came the earlier formularies themselves, from which Cranmer and the rest quarried the stone for the new building ?—to change the metaphor as Paul, you remember, does so suddenly from husbandry to architecture.* Whence came Missal, and Breviary, and Book of Offices—the best portions of which were merged in the English Common Prayer ? From the far past, the Missal from those primitive liturgies or communion services, some of which we trace back with certainty to the later portion of the ante-Nicene age, and by not unreasonable conjecture to the edge of apostolic days; the Breviary or daily prayers from the times when Christians first took up community life; the Offices from periods of uncertain date all along the track of previous Church history. But what advantage, asks someone full of the modern spirit, what advantage has the Common Prayer in that it can trace a genealogy running up through ages of such uncertain reputation ? Have we not been accustomed to regard those times as hopelessly corrupt, impenetrably dark, universally superstitious ? Ought we not to be mortified, rather than gratified, to learn that from the pit of so mouldy a past our book of prayer was digged ? Would not a brand-new liturgy, modernized expressly to meet the needs of nineteenth century culture, with all

* 1 Cor. iii. 9

the old English idioms displaced, every rough corner smoothed and every crooked place made straight—would not that be something far worthier our respect, better entitled to our allegiance, than this book full of far-away echoes, and faint bell-notes from a half-forgotten past?

Yes, if modern man were only modern man and nothing more, such reasoning would be extremely cogent. But what if modern man be really, not the mere creature of the century in which he lives, but the gathered sum and product of all that has preceded him in history? What if you and I, from the very fact that we are living now, have in the dim groundwork of our nature something that would not have been there had we lived one, three, twelve hundred years ago? What if there be such a thing as cumulative acquirement for the race of men, so that a new generation starts with an available capital of associations and ideas of which the generation last preceding it owned but a part? Take such words as "feudalism," "the Crusades," "the Renaissance," "the printing press," consider how much they mean to us, and then remember that to a man of the third century they would have been empty sounds conveying absolutely no meaning. What all this goes to show is that human nature is a map which is continually unrolling. To say that the entirety of it lies between the two meridians that bound the particular tract in which our own little life happens to be cast is stupid. The whole great past belongs to us—river and island, ocean, forest, continent, all are ours. You and the man in armor, you and the Venetian merchant, you and the cowled monk have something, be it ever so little, something in common. That which was in the foreground of their life is now in the background or in the middle distance of yours. It has become a part of you.*

> * Born into life !—man grows
> Forth from his parents' stem,
> And blends their bloods, as those
> Of theirs are blent in them ;
> So each new man strikes root into a far fore time.
>
> Born into life !—we bring
> A bias with us here,
> And, when here, each new thing
> Affects us as we come near ;
> To tunes we did not call our being must keep chime
> —*Empedocles on Etna*

APPENDIX. 217

So, then, if we would have a liturgy that shall speak to our whole nature, and not to a mere fraction of it, it must be a liturgy full of voices sounding out of the past. There must be reminders and suggestions in it of all the great epochs of the Church's story Yes, echoes even from those very ages which we call dark (perhaps as much because we are in the dark about them as on account of any special blackness attaching to the times themselves), some echoes even from them may have a rightful place in the worship which is to call out responsively all that is in the heart of the most modern of modern men

As there were heroes before Agamemnon, so were there holy and humble men of heart before Cranmer and Luther, yes, and before Jerome and Augustine If any cry that ever went up from any one of them out of the depths of that nature which they share with us and we with them, if any breath of supplication, any moan of penitence, any shout of victory that issued from their lips has made out to survive the noise and tumult of intervening times, it has earned by its very persistency of tone a *prima facie* title to be put into the Prayer Book of to-day.* And this is why a prayer book may survive the wreck of many systems of theology. A prayer book holds the utterance of our needs ; a theological system is the embodiment of our thoughts

Now our thoughts about things divine are painfully fallible and liable to change with change of times ; but a want which is genuinely and entirely human is a permanent fact ; the great needs of the soul never grow obsolete, and though the language in which the lips shall clothe the heart's desire may alter, as tastes alter, yet the substance of the prayer abides, and in some happy instances the form also abides.

To an eye that looks wisely and lovingly on such sights, there is the same keen sense of enjoyment in finding here and there in

---

* " Parliaments, prelates, convocations, synods may order forms of prayer They may get speeches to be spoken upward by people on their knees. They may obtain a juxtaposition in space of curiously tessellated pieces of Bible and Prayer Book But when I speak of the rareness and preciousness of prayers, I mean such prayers as contain three conditions—permanence, capability of being really prayed, and universality Such prayers primates and senates can no more command than they can order a new Cologne Cathedral or another epic poem."—*The Bishop of Derry's Bampton Lectures*, lect iv.

the Prayer Book suggestions of forgotten customs, reminders of famous persons and events, that there is in detecting in the masonry of an old castle or minster tell-tale stones which betray the different ages, the "sundry times and divers manners" which the fabric represents. Who, for instance, that has traced the history of that apostolic ordinance, "the kiss of peace," down through the liturgical changes and revolutions of eighteen hundred years, can fail to be interested in finding in a single clause of one of the exhortations of our communion service that which corresponds to the literal kiss of primitive times, as well as to the petrified symbol of the original reality, the silver, ivory, or wooden "osculatory" of the mediæval Church?* So with "Ash-Wednesday," a single syllable opens a whole chapter of Church history. Again, the Latin headings to the psalms of the Psalter; with what an impatient gesture can we imagine a spruce reviser brushing these away as so much trash! They are not trash, they are waymarks that tell of times when devout men loved those catchwords, as we love

* The following *catena* is curious:
"Salute one another with an holy kiss"—Rom. xvi. 10.
"Greet ye one another with a kiss of charity."—1 Pet. v. 14.
"*And let the bishop salute the church, and say* Let the peace of God be with you all.
"*And let the people answer*, And with thy spirit.
"*And let the deacon say to all*, Salute one another with a holy kiss.
"*And let the clergy kiss the bishop; and of the laity, the men the men, and the women the women, and let the children stand by the Bema.*"—The *Divine Liturgy of St. Clement* (Brett's Translation, corrected by Neale).
"¶ *At Solemn High Mass, the deacon kisses the altar at the same time with the celebrating priest, by whom he is saluted with the kiss of peace, accompanied by these words,* PAX TECUM."—*Rubric of the Roman Missal.*
"PAX OR PAXBREDE. A small plate of gold, or silver, or copper-gilt, enamelled, or piece of carved ivory or wood overlaid with metal, carried round, having been kissed by the priest, after the Agnus Dei in the Mass, to communicate the kiss of peace"—*Pugin's Glossary.*

St. George's Chapel, Windsor "Item, a fine Pax, silver and gilt enamelled, with an image of the crucifixion, Mary and John, and having on the top three crosses, with two shields hanging on either side. Item, a ferial Pax, of plate of silver gilt, with the image of the Blessed Virgin"—*Dugdale's Monasticon* quoted in above Glossary.

"Ye who do truly and earnestly repent you of your sins, *and are in love and charity with your neighbors,* and intend to lead a new life. . . Draw near with faith, and take this holy sacrament to your comfort."—Shorter Exhortation in the Communion Office of the Prayer Book.

the first lines of our favorite hymns. A few of the headings, such as "*De Profundis*" and "*Miserere,*" still possess such associations for ourselves. There was a time when very many more of them meant to men now dead and gone as much as "Rock of Ages," or "Sun of my Soul," or "Lead, kindly Light," can mean to you or me.*

Then, too, the monuments of specially revered heroes of the faith that dot the paths of the Common Prayer, how precious they are! We like to think of Ambrose as speaking to us in the lofty sentences of the *Te Deum*. It is pleasant to associate Chrysostom with the prayer that bears his name, and to know that he who swayed the city's multitude still prized the Master's promise to the "two or three gathered together" in his name. So also, in our American Book, Jeremy Taylor, the modern Chrysostom, meets us in the Office for the Visitation of the Sick, in that solemn prayer addressed to Him " whose days are without end, and whose mercies cannot be numbered." All these things help to make the Prayer Book the large-hearted, wide-minded book we all of us feel it to be, so like a friend whom we revere because he is kindly in his tone, generous in his judgments, quick to understand us at every point.

So much for the past of the Prayer Book. We have touched it in no image-breaking mood, but with reverence. "One generation passeth away, another generation cometh," and it has been the peculiar felicity of this book to stand

> A link among the days, to knit
> The generations each to each.

We pass on to consider the present usefulness of the Prayer

---

* A friend who heard the sermon preached has kindly sent me the following apt illustrations. They do not, indeed, come from history technically so-called, but they report the mind of one to whose eye the whole life of the Middle Ages was as an open book.

"There was now a pause, of which the abbot availed himself by commanding the brotherhood to raise the solemn chant, *De profundis clamavi*"—*The Monastery,* chap. xxxvii.

"'To be a guest in the house where I should command?' said the Templar, 'Never! Chaplains, raise the psalm, *Quare fremuerunt Gentes?* Knights, squires, and followers of the Holy Temple, prepare to follow the banner of *Beau-seant!*'"—*Ivanhoe,* chap. xliv.

Book and the possibility of extending that usefulness in the future. And now I shall speak wholly as an American to Americans, not because the destinies of the Prayer Book in the New World are the more important, though such may in the end turn out to be the fact, but simply because we are at home here and know our own wants and wishes, our own liabilities and opportunities, far better than we can possibly know those of other people. As a Church we have always tied ourselves too slavishly to English precedent. Our vine is greatly in danger of continuing merely a potted ivy, an indoor exotic. The past of the Common Prayer we cannot disconnect from England, but its present and its future belong in part at least to us, and it is in this light that we are bound as American Churchmen to study them. Let us agree, then, that the usefulness of the book here and now lies largely in the moulding and formative influence which it is quietly exerting, not only on the religion of those who use it, but also largely on the religion of the far greater number who publicly use it not. It has interested me, as it would interest almost anyone, to learn how many prayer books our booksellers supply to Christian people who are not Churchmen. Evidently the book is in use as a private manual with thousands, who own no open allegiance to the Protestant Episcopal Church. They keep it on the devotional shelf midway between Thomas à Kempis and the Pilgrim's Progress, finding it a sort of interpreter of the one to the other, and possessed of a certain flavor differencing it from both. This is a happy augury for the future. Much latent heat is generating which shall yet warm up the chillness of the land. The seed-grain of the Common Prayer will not lie unproductive in those forgotten furrows. The fitness of such a system of worship as this to counteract some of the flagrant evils of our popular religion can scarcely fail to commend it to the minds of those who thus unobserved and, "as it were in secret," read and ponder. Much of our American piety, fervid as it is, shows confessedly a feverish, intermittent character which needs just such a tonic as the Prayer Book provides in what Keble happily called its "sober standard of feeling in matters of practical religion."

Then, too, there is the constantly increasing interest which it is such a pleasure to observe among Christians of all names in the order of the ritual year, in Christmas and Easter, Lent and Good-Friday—who can tell how much of this may not be due to the leavening influence of the Prayer Book, over and above what is effected by the public services of the Church? "I wonder," said a famous revivalist to a friend, a clergyman of our Church, "I wonder if you Episcopalians know what a good thing you have in that year of yours. Why don't you use it more?"

And true enough, why do we not? That we might learn to do so was a wish very near to the heart of that holy and true man who, if anyone, deserves the title of the saint among our priests, the late Dr. Muhlenberg, the man who twenty-five years ago headed the not wholly abortive movement known as the "Memorial." * One fruit of that movement is perhaps to be seen in the earnest desire now prevalent throughout the Church to see the scope of the Prayer Book's influence enlarged. In General Conventions and Church Congresses nowadays no topic excites greater interest than the question how better to adapt the services of the Church to the present needs and special conditions of all classes of the population. To be sure, the apparent impotence of the govern-

* So many good things are washed out of men's memory by the lapse of even a quarter of a century that possibly some even of those who knew all about the "Memorial" in 1852 may be willing to be reminded what its scope and purpose were.

The petition was addressed to the bishops "in council," and prayed for the appointment of a commission to report upon the practicability of making this Church a central bond of union among the Christian people of America, by providing for as much freedom in opinion, discipline, and worship as might be held to be compatible with the essential faith and order of the Gospel.

The desired commission was appointed, Bishops Otey, Doane, A. Potter, Burgess, and Williams being the members of it. Their Report, subsequently edited in book form by Bishop Potter, is one of the most valuable documents of American Church history. The following extract from Bishop Burgess' portion of the Report will be read with interest by all who ever learned to revere that theologian for the largeness of his learning, the calmness of his judgment, and the goodness of his heart. He has been speaking of liturgical changes as contemplated and allowed for by the framers of our ecclesiastical system. Then he says:

"There would seem to be five contingencies in which the changes, thus made possible and thus permitted, become also wise and salutary.

"The first is simply when it is evident that in any respect the liturgy or its application may be rendered more perfect. To hazard for this result the safety or unity of the Church may be inexcusable, and the utmost certainty may be

ing body to find or furnish any lawful way of relief is a little discouraging, but it is something to see an almost universal assent given in terms, to the proposition that relief ought to be had. What we have to fear is that during the long delay which puts off the only proper and regular method of giving more elasticity to the services, there may spring up a generation of Churchmen from whose minds the idea of obligation to law in matters of ritual observance will have faded out altogether.

There is a conservatism so conservative that it will stand by and see a building tumble down rather than lay a sacrilegious hand on a single stone, will see dam and mill and village all swept away sooner than lift the flash-boards that keep the superabundant water from coming safely down. It is among the things possible, that for lack of readjustment and timely adaptation of the laws regulating worship, just such a fate may befall our whole liturgical fabric.

The plausible theory of "the rubric of common sense," about which we have heard so much, a theory good within limitations, is threatening, by the wholesale application it receives, presently

demanded before a change of this kind shall be practically ventured But should it be once established, beyond the smallest doubt, that any addition or alteration would increase the excellence or the excellent influence of the liturgy in any degree sufficient to compensate or more than compensate for the inconveniences incident to all change, it seems as difficult to say that it should not be adopted by the Church, as to excuse any Christian from adding to his virtues or his usefulness

"The other 'contingencies' recognized are briefly these:

"(2) When in process of time words or regulations have become obsolete or unsuitable

"(3) When civil or social changes require ecclesiastical changes

"(4) When the earnest desire of any respectable number of the members of the Church, or of persons who are without its communion, is urged in behalf of some not wholly unreasonable proposal of alteration.

"(5) When error or superstition has been introduced; when that which was at first good and healthful has been perverted to the nourishment of falsehood or wickedness; or when that which was always evil has found utterance, and is now revealed in its true character."

The Memorial failed for the reason that the promoters of it had not a clearly defined notion in their own minds of what they wanted—the secret of many failures. Out of its ashes there may yet rise, however, "some better thing" that God has kept in store.

to annul all other rubrics whatsoever. When, by this process, uniformity and even similarity shall have been utterly abolished, when it shall have become impossible for one to know beforehand of a Sunday whether he is going to mass, or to meeting, or to church, the inquiry will be in order, What has conservatism of this sort really conserved ?

"The personal liberty of the officiating clergyman," I fear will be the only answer ; certainly not, "The liberty of the worshipping congregation." The straight and only honest way out of our embarrassment will, some day or other, be found, I dare not believe very soon, in a careful, loving, fair-minded revision of the formularies ; a revision undertaken, not for the purpose of giving victory to one theological party rather than to another, or of changing in any degree the doctrinal teaching of the Church, but solely and wholly with a view to enriching, amplifying, and making more available the liturgical treasures of the book.

"One generation passeth away, another generation cometh" As we have seen in these words an argument in favor of not breaking with the past, so let them also speak to us of our plain duty to the present. True, the great needs are, as I have said, common alike to all the generations, to those that pass and those that come; but the lesser needs are variable, and unless we are prepared to take the ground that because "lesser" they may be disregarded altogether, we are bound, with the changed times, to provide for the new wants new satisfactions. Take, simply by way of illustration, the need we stand in of an appropriate form of third service for use on Sundays in city churches, when Morning and Evening Prayer have been already said according to the prescribed order.

Why have we no such service ?

Simply because no such need existed in our American cities when the Prayer Book, as we have it now, was taking shape, at the close of the last century. Just as no form for the administration of Adult Baptism was put into Queen Elizabeth's Prayer Book, simply because the usage of Infant Baptism was universal in that day, and there were no unbaptized adults ; but such service was inserted at the Restoration to meet the need that had sprung up under the Puritan regime ; so was it unnecessary in Bishop White's day to provide for a form of service which has only become practicable and desirable since modern discovery has enabled us to make the public streets almost as safe at night as in the daytime, and church-going as easy by gaslight as by sunlight.

Now it is perfectly possible, of course, under the present order of things, and with no change in rubric or canon law, for any clergyman to provide an additional service, to provide it in the form of a mosaic made up of bits of the liturgy wrenched out of their proper places, and so irregularly put together that no stranger among the worshippers can possibly, with the book in hand, thread his way among its intricacies.

But when we consider how many exquisite gems of devotional speech there are still left outside the covers of the Prayer Book; when we consider how delightful it would be to have back again the *Magnificat*, and the *Nunc Dimittis*, and some of the sweet versicles of the Evensong of the Church of England; when we consider the lamentable mistake already made in our existing formularies of introducing into Morning and Evening Prayer identically the same opening sentences, the same General Exhortation, the same General Confession, the same Declaration of Absolution, the same Prayer for the President, and the same General Thanksgiving—is it not evident that an additional, or, if you please, an alternative service, composed of material not elsewhere employed, would be for the worshippers a very great gain? The repetition which wearies is only the repetition which we feel need not have been. We never tire of the Collect for Peace any more than we tire of the sunset. It is in its place, and we always welcome it. In a perfect liturgy no form of words, except the Creed, the Doxology, and the Lord's Prayer, would at any time reappear, but as in arabesque work every square inch of space differs from every other square, so each clause and sentence of the manual of worship would have a distinctive beauty of its own, to be looked for precisely there and nowhere else.

This is but one illustration of what may be called a possible enrichment of our Book of Common Prayer. Impoverishment under the name of revision may very justly be deprecated, but who shall find any just fault with an enrichment that is really such?

We must remember that the men who gave us what we now have were, in their day and generation, the innovators, advocates of what the more timid spirits accounted dangerous change. We cannot, I think, sufficiently admire the courageous foresight of those Reformers who, at a time when public worship was mainly associated in men's minds with what went on among a number of ecclesiastics gathered together at one end of a church, dared to plant themselves firmly on the principle of "common" prayer, and to say, Henceforth the worship of the National Church shall be the worship not of priests alone, but of priests and people too What a bold act it was ! The printing-press, remember, although it had given the impulse to the Reformation, was far from being at that time the omnipresent thing it is now ; books were scarce, popular education, as we understand it, was unknown ; there were no means of supplying service-books to the poorer classes (no Prayer Book Societies, like this of yours), nor could the books have been used had they been furnished. And yet in the face of these seemingly insuperable obstacles, the leaders of religious thought in the England of that day had the sagacity to plan a system of worship which should involve participation by the people in all the acts of divine service, including the administration of the sacraments.

Here was genuine statesmanship applied to the administration of religion Those men discerned wisely the signs of their own times. They saw what the right principle was, they foresaw what the art of printing was destined in time to accomplish, and they did a piece of work which has bravely stood the wear and tear of full three hundred years

No Churchman questions the wisdom of their innovations now. Is it hopeless to expect a like quickness of discernment in the leaders of to-day ? Surely they have eyes to see that a new world has been born, and that a thousand unexampled demands are pressing us on every side. If the Prayer Book is not enriched with a view to meeting those demands, it is not for lack of materials. A Saturday reviewer has tried to fasten on the Church of England the stigma of being the Church which for the space of two centuries has not been able to evolve a fresh prayer.

If the reproach were just it would be stinging indeed ; but it is most cruelly unjust In the devotional literature of the Anglicanism of the last fifty years, to go no further back, there may be found prayers fully equal in compass of thought and depth of feeling to any of those that are already in public use. Not to single out too many instances, it may suffice to mention the prayers appended to the book of *Ancient Collects* edited a few years since by a distinguished Oxford scholar. The clergy are acquainted with them, and know how beautiful they are. Why should not the whole Church enjoy the happiness of using them? * Why is there not the same propriety in our garnering the devotional harvest of the three hundred years last past that there was in the Reformers garnering the harvest of five times three hundred years?

"One generation passeth away, another generation cometh." I have spoken of the present and the past, what now of the

---

* *Ancient Collects and Other Prayers selected for Devotional Use from Various Rituals.* By William Bright, M A. J H. & Jas. Parker, Oxford and London.

From the Appendix I take the following illustrations of the statement ventured above:

"*For Guidance.*—O God, by whom the meek are guided in judgment, and light riseth up in darkness for the godly; grant us in all our doubts and uncertainties the grace to ask what thou wouldest have us to do; that the Spirit of wisdom may save us from all false choices, and that in thy light we may see light, and in thy straight path may not stumble: through Jesus Christ our Lord.

"*For those who live in sin.*—Have mercy, O compassionate Father, on all who are hardened through the deceitfulness of sin; vouchsafe them grace to come to themselves, the will and power to return to thee, and the loving welcome of thy forgiveness through Jesus Christ our Lord.

"*For all who do the work of the Church.*—O Lord, without whom our labor is but lost, and with whom thy little ones go forth as the mighty, be present to all works in thy Church which are undertaken according to thy will, and grant to thy laborers a pure intention, patient faith, sufficient success upon earth, and the bliss of serving thee in heaven, through Jesus Christ our Lord.

"*For grace to speak the Truth in love.*—O Lord and Saviour Jesus Christ, who camest not to strive nor cry, but to let thy words fall as the drops that water the earth: grant all who contend for the faith once delivered, never to injure it by clamor and impatience, but speaking thy precious truth in love, so to present it that it may be loved, and that men may see in it thy goodness and thy beauty: who livest and reignest with the Father and the Holy Ghost, one God, world without end."

Both as regards devotional flavor and literary beauty these prayers will, I feel sure, be judged worthy, by such as will read them more than once, to stand by the side certainly of many of the collects already in the Prayer Book.

future ? We know that all things come to an end. What destiny awaits the book to which our evening thoughts have been given ? That is a path not open to our tread. The cloudy curtain screens the threshold of it Still we may listen and imagine that we hear sounds. What if such a voice as this were to come to us from the distance of a hundred years hence—a voice tinged with sadness, and carrying just the least suggestion of reproach ? "Our fathers," the voice says, "in the last quarter of the last century, forfeited a golden opportunity. It was a time of reconstruction in the State, social life was taking on the form it was destined long to retain, a great war had come to an end and its results were being registered, all things were fluent. Moreover, there happened, just then, to be an almost unparalleled lull in the strife of religious parties ; men were more disposed than usual to agree ; the interest in liturgical research was at its greatest, and scholars knew and cared more than they have ever done since about the history and the structure of forms of prayer. Nevertheless, timid councils prevailed ; nothing was done with a view to better adapting the system to the needs of society, and the hope that the Church might cease to wear the dimensions of a sect, and might become the chosen home of a great people, died unrealized. We struggle on, a half-hearted company, and try to live upon the high traditions, the sweet memories of our past."

God forbid, my friends, that the dismal prophecy come true ! We will not believe it. But what, you ask, is the pathway to any such betterment as I have ventured roughly to sketch to-night ? I will not attempt to map it, but I feel very confident which way it does not run I am sure it does not run through the region of disaffection, complaint, threatening, restlessness, petulance, or secession Mere fretfulness never carries its points. No, the true way to better things is always to begin by holding on manfully to that which we already are convinced is good. The best restorers of old fabrics are those who work with affectionate loyalty as nearly as possible on the lines of the first builders, averse to any change which is made merely for change's sake, not so anxious to modernize as to restore, and yet always awake to the fact that what they have been set to do is to make the building once more what it was first meant to be, a practicable shelter

THE OUTCOME OF REVISION—A SERMON *

" . . . We are the servants of the God of heaven and earth, and build the house that was builded these many years ago."—Ezra v. 11.

This was the reply of the rebuilders of Jerusalem to certain critical lookers-on who would fain be informed by what authority a picturesque ruin was disturbed. It is a serviceable answer still. There are always those to whom the activity of the Christian Church is a standing puzzle. Religion, or at any rate revealed religion, having, as they think, received its death-blow, the unmistakable signs of life which, from time to time, it manifests take on almost the character of a personal affront. They resent them. What right have these Christians to be showing such a lively interest in their vanquished faith? they ask. What business have they to be holding councils, and laying plans, and acting as if they had some high and splendid effort in hand? Are they such fools as to imagine that they can reconstruct what has so evidently tumbled into ruin?

But the wonderful thing about this great building enterprise known as the kingdom of God is that, from the day when the corner-stone was laid to this day, the workmen on the walls have never seemed to know what it meant to be discouraged. In the face of taunt and rebuff and disappointment, they have kept on saying to their critics: "We are the servants of the God of heaven and earth, and build the house that was builded these many years ago." This is just what the Church Council which has been holding its sessions in Baltimore during the last three weeks has to say for itself. Its task has been an architectural task. According to its lights, it has been at work upon the walls of the city of God. Let me give you, as my habit has been under similar circumstances in the past, some account of its doings.

* Preached in Grace Church, N. Y., on the Twentieth Sunday after Trinity, that being the Sunday next following the adjournment of the General Convention of 1892.

The General Convention of 1892 will be memorable in our ecclesiastical annals for having closed one question of grave moment only to open a kindred one of still larger reach. The question closed was the question of liturgical revision; the question opened is the question of constitutional revision. I should like to speak to you this morning retrospectively of the one, and prospectively of the other.

It is now about twenty years since the question of modifying, to some extent, the methods of our public worship began to be mooted.

While it was acknowledged that the need was greater in the mother country than here, many of the repetitions and superfluities of the English Church service having been set aside by Bishop White and his compeers in the American Revision of 1789, it was felt that further improvements were still possible, and that the time had fully come for making them. Since the beginning of the so-called "tractarian movement" in the Church of England a great deal of valuable liturgical material had been accumulating, and it was discerned that if ever the fruits of the scholarship of such men as Palmer and Neale and Maskell and Bright were to be garnered the harvest-day had arrived. To the question often asked why it would not have been wiser to wait until the Church of England had led the way and set the pattern, the answer is that the hands of the Church of England were tied, as they have been tied these many years past, and as they may continue to be tied, for aught we know to the contrary, for many years to come The Church of England cannot touch her own Prayer Book, whether to mend or to mar it, except with the consent of that very mixed body, the House of Commons—a consent she is naturally and properly most loth to ask. Immersed in a veritable ocean of accumulated liturgical material, she is as helpless as Tantalus to moisten her lips with so much as a single drop. It was seen that this fact laid upon us American Churchmen a responsibility as urgent as it was unique, viz., the responsibility of doing what we could to meet the devotional needs of present-day Christendom, not only for our own advantage, but with a view to being ultimately of service to our Anglican brethren across the sea. An experiment of the greatest interest, which for them was a sheer impossibility, it lay open to us to try. After various abortive attempts had come to nought, a beginning was at length made in the General Convention of 1880, a joint committee of bishops and deputies being then appointed to consider whether, in view of the fact that this Church was soon to enter upon the second century of its organized existence in America, the changed condition of the national life did not demand certain alterations in the Book of Common Prayer in the direction of liturgical enrichment and increased flexibility of use.

Few were of the opinion at the time that anything definite would come of the deliberations of this committee, and the fact, never before publicly stated till this moment, that of the deputies appointed to serve upon it the greater number were men who had not voted in favor of the measure, makes it all the more interesting to remember that the report, when brought in at Philadelphia three years later, was signed by every member of the committee then living. This Philadelphia report recommended very numerous changes in the direction both of "flexibility" and "enrichment," and by far the greater number of the recommendations met with the approval of the convention. There is, however, a very wise provision of our Church constitution, a provision strikingly characteristic of the Anglo-Saxon mind, which, by way of making allowance for second thought, requires that liturgical changes, before being finally adopted, shall run the gauntlet of two successive conventions. Much was accepted at Philadelphia; it remained to be seen how much would pass the ordeal of its second reading at Chicago three years later.

Into the war of words waged over the subject during that interval period, I have neither the time nor the disposition to carry you The three years, while they gave opportunity for reaction, also allowed space for counter-reaction; so that when, at last, the question came once more before the Church in council assembled whether the work done at Philadelphia should be approved or disallowed, men's minds had sufficiently recovered balance to permit of their exercising discrimination. Accordingly in 1886 some things were rejected, some adopted, and some remanded for further revision But why should I confuse your minds by an attempt to tell in detail the whole story of the movement ? No matter how clear I might make the narrative it would be difficult to follow it, for in the progress of the work there have been surprises many, successes and reverses not a few; enough that, at last, the long labor is ended and in this Columbian year the ship comes into port

As to results, their number and their quality, opinions will of course differ. In connection with this, as with all similar undertakings, there are many to cry : "Who will show us any good ?" Certainly nothing that could be called a radical change has been brought to pass; but then, is there any reason to suppose that radical changes were either sought or desired by those who have been active in the movement ? Certain distinct and indisputable gains may be counted up. The recovery of the great Gospel hymns come under this head. There are some of us who think that only to have succeeded in replacing the *Magnificat* and the *Nunc Dimittis* in the Evening Prayer is of itself a sufficient reward for years of effort, but this is only a small part of our harvest. The new opening sentences for Morning and Evening Prayer, which have so "adorned and beautified" our observance of great festivals, the remodelling of the Ash-Wednesday service, the recovered Feast of the Transfiguration, the various provisions for adapting the Church's worship to the exigencies of times and seasons, the increased freedom in the use of the Psalter, all these go to make up an aggregate of betterment the measure of which will be more fully understood as time goes on. "*Parturiunt montes*" is an easy verdict to pronounce; it remains to be proved whether in this case it is a just one to render. If there are some (as doubtless some there are) who hold that the sample book presented at Philadelphia in 1883, faulty as it confessedly was, is still, all things considered, a better book for American needs than the standard finally adopted at Baltimore, week before last, if there are some who deeply regret the failure to include among our special offices one for the burial of little children, and among our prayers intercessions for the country, for the families of the land, for schools of good learning, for employers and those whom they employ, together with many other forms of supplication gathered from the wide field of English liturgiology—if, I say, there are some who are of this mind they must comfort themselves with the reflection that, after all, they are a minority, that the greater number of those upon whom rested the responsibility of decision did not wish for these additions, and that the things which finally found acceptance were the things unanimously desired. For, when we think of it, this is perhaps the very best feature of the whole thing, looked at in its length and breadth, that there is no defeated party, no body of people who feel that they have a right to fret and sulk because unpalatable changes have been forced upon them by narrow majorities. It is a remarkable fact, that of the many scores of alterations effected, it can be truly said that, with rare, very rare exceptions, they found, when it came to the decisive vote, what was practically a unanimous consent. They were things that everybody wanted.

As to the annoyance and vexation experienced by worshippers during the years the revision has been in progress, perhaps the very best thing that can be done, now that the end is so near at hand, will be to forget all about it. In a few months, at the furthest, the Prayer Book, in its complete form, will be available for purchase and use, and the hybrid copies which have been so long in circulation, to the scandal of people of fastidious taste, will quickly vanish away. Meanwhile, it is interesting to know that all through this stretch of years while the Prayer Book has been "in solution," as some have been fond of phrasing it, the Episcopal Church has exhibited a rate of growth quite unparalleled in its history.

Of course nobody can say with certainty what has caused the increase. But it is at least conceivable that among the accelerating forces has been this very work of liturgical revision. People at large have been made aware that this Church was honestly endeavoring to adapt its system of worship to the needs of our time and country ; and the mere fact of their seeing this to be the case has served to allay prejudice and to foster a spirit of inquiry. Finding us disposed to relax something of our rigidity, they, on their part, have been first attracted, then conciliated, and finally completely won.

I cannot leave this subject without paying a personal tribute to a prelate but for whose aid in the House of which he is a distinguished ornament, liturgical revision would, humanly speaking, have long ago come to nought To the fearlessness, the patience, the kindly temper, and the resolute purpose of William Croswell Doane, Bishop of Albany, this Church for these results stands deeply and lastingly indebted When others' courage failed them, he stood firm ; when friends and colleagues were counselling retreat, and under their breath were whispering "Fiasco !" and "Collapse !" his spirit never faltered. He has been true to a great purpose, at the cost of obloquy sometimes, and to the detriment even of old friendships. Separated from him by a dozen shades of theological opinion and by as many degrees of ecclesiastical bias, I render him here and now that homage of grateful appreciation which every Churchman owes him.

So much for the ship that has dropped anchor. I have left myself but a few moments in which to say God-speed to the other craft which is even now sliding down the ways, ready for the great deep. But perhaps it is just as well History is always a safer line to enter upon than prophecy , and were I to say all that is in my mind and heart as to the possibilities of this new venture of faith on the Church's part, constitutional revision, I might be betrayed into expressions of hopefulness which would strike most of you as overwrought.

Suffice it to say, that never since the Reformation of Religion in the sixteenth century has a fairer prospect been opened to the Church of our affections than is opened to her to day. No interpretation of the divine purpose with respect to this broad land we name America has one-half so much of likelihood as that which makes our country the predestined building plot for the Church of the Reconciliation

All signs point that way. To us, if we have but the eyes to see it, there falls, not through any merit of our own, but by the accident, if it be right to use that word, by the accident of historical association, the opportunity of leadership

It is possible for us, at this crisis of our destiny, so to mould our organic law that we shall be brought into sympathetic contact with hundreds of thousands of our fellow-countrymen who worship the same God, hold the same faith, love the same Christ. On the other hand, it is possible for us so to fence ourselves off from this huge family of our fellow-believers as to secure for our lasting heritage only the cold privileges of a proud and selfish isolation. There could be no real catholicity in such a choice as that.

We have the opportunity of growing into a great and comprehensive Church We have the opportunity of dwindling into a self-conscious, self-conceited, and unsympathetic sect Which shall it be ? With those to whom, under God, the remoulding of our organic law has been intrusted it largely rests to say.

APPENDIX. 235

Comparative Table of Additions made to the Book of Common Prayer at the Several Revisions since 1549.

	1552	1559	1604	1662	1789	1892
Scripture Sentences	11	.	.	.	8	31
Collects	.	.	.	3	1	3
Epistles	.	.	.	2	1	3
Gospels	.	.	.	1	1	3
Offices	13	.	.	8	1	1
Prayers	15	2	7	18	13	9
Proper Psalms (days)	.	.	.	2	.	10
Selections of Psalms	.	.	.	.	10	10
Canticles	3	.	.	.	8	2
Versicles	4	.	.	3	.	11
Litany, Suffrages	.	.	1	.	.	1
Catechetical Questions	.	.	12	.	.	.
Exhortations	3	.	.	2	.	.

BIBLIOLIFE

Old Books Deserve a New Life
www.bibliolife.com

Did you know that you can get most of our titles in our trademark **EasyScript**™ print format? **EasyScript**™ provides readers with a larger than average typeface, for a reading experience that's easier on the eyes.

Did you know that we have an ever-growing collection of books in many languages?

Order online:
www.bibliolife.com/store

Or to exclusively browse our **EasyScript**™ collection:
www.bibliogrande.com

At BiblioLife, we aim to make knowledge more accessible by making thousands of titles available to you – quickly and affordably.

Contact us:
BiblioLife
PO Box 21206
Charleston, SC 29413